POTLATCH

POTLATCH

GEORGE CLUTESI

Illustrations by the Author

GRAY'S PUBLISHING LTD., SIDNEY, BRITISH COLUMBIA, CANADA

First printing May 1969
Second printing August 1969
Third printing May 1971
This edition 1973

I.S.B.N. 0 - 88826 - 046 - 6

PRINTED IN CANADA

This narrative is not meant to be documentary. In fact it is meant to evade documents. It is meant for the reader to feel and to say I was there and indeed I saw.

GEORGE CLUTESI

DEDICATION

This book I dedicate to my sister, Anne,
without whose help and information this
book would not have been.

GEORGE CLUTESI

INTRODUCTION

THE AUTHOR OF THIS STORY attended and participated in the last Tloo-qwah-nah when he was a very young man. It was then unlawful to entertain a feast or a potlatch by a decree of the Indian Act. Indeed his own kin was arrested for having staged such a Tloo-qwah-nah. It is then with trepidations that this "eye-witness" account is given and it is because of this lingering fear that actual names have been omitted.

To spare the reader monotonous repetitions the writer has purposely contrived to omit many dances and the subsequent gift giving during the progress of the Tloo-qwah-nah but instead has endeavoured to bring forth and dramatize outstanding performances. It may be sufficient to say that each song and dance would be followed by the gifts from those doing each entertainment. The verses are translations, as far as possible, of traditional speeches.

Feasts were classified in four categories.

He-nim-tsu . . . guests consisted of club members.

Tlee-dtsoo . . . included members of the home tribe.

Hutch-yahk . . . the host journeyed to another tribe to give a feast.

Tloo-qwah-nah . . . guests were invited from any number of tribes.

Tloo-qwah-nah later came to be known as Potlatch by the early Europeans perhaps because the Nootka verb Pa-chitle, to give, was often heard during these festivities so naturally the early settlers mistook that verb for the name of the feast. Pa-chitle is the verb. Pa-chuck is the noun and means article to be given. Both words were used only when the articles were given in public such as at a feast.

Almost any person, including women, could give as many feasts as they wished but were not expected to stage more than one Tloo-qwah-nah. It was through this practice of sharing that the society of the Tloo-qwah-nah came into being. The initiatory ceremonies required to gain its portals were imposing and extremely costly but nevertheless all *bona fide* members of all the tribes along the west coast of the great Island, Vancouver Island, belonged to the Tloo-qwah-nah Society. It was known to be the most powerful society that flourished along this rugged coast.

For years prior to a Tloo-qwah-nah the principal and his councillors began to plan and to accumulate various articles that he would give away — sea-otter robes; whaling canoes, sleek sea-otter and fur-seal hunting canoes and the smaller fishing and utility canoes. These canoes required harpoons, lanyards, thongs, buoys, paddles, spears, bailers, water containers, paints and pigments with which to treat and preserve them. Then there were the smaller articles such as cooking utensils and chattels of many kinds.

The most important gift one could give was the bestowal of a song together with its dance and the ornate paraphernalia needed to show any subsequent ceremonial presentations.

Territories, fishing and hunting rights and the right to keep all game caught within these territories and all flotsam found therein was on extraordinary occasions included in the bestowal of gifts and only then was the recipient able to give a feast in his own name. He was also granted a place in the seating arrangement of guests and so became eligible for a subsequent seat in the senate.

When the business of estimating of goods and chattels began all members and relatives of the prospective host were honor bound to help in every way possible. Let it be understood that all guests had to be housed and fed throughout the entire duration of a Tloo-qwah-nah which must last at least fourteen days or a maximum of twenty-eight days, the full phase of a moon.

All undertakings of importance in this society were begun at a crescent moon and were obliged to advance at least to the half moon. This law was strictly conformed to. All hunters of the House eagerly went out and stayed out to bring down the game from the forests and hills while the younger men, who were not yet accepted as hunters, brought and packed the carcasses down to the lodge where the older men and the womenfolk butchered them in preparation for the quick-roast over a hot fire that would follow. That helped to preserve it for future use. Fishermen and hunters went to sea to bring home the wealth of foodstuff it afforded.

The old men were useful in keeping the wood pile replenished. They gathered their supply from known beaches that abounded with driftwood carried in by the tides and left high and dry above normal high-water-mark. Young boys, too, at this time of the season loved to pack the wood indoors in preparation for the coming great event while the young girls watched and poked at the fires to marvel at the myriad of live sparkling stars that floated upward on invisible surges of air currents to effuse through the smoke-hole at the ridge of the easy sloping plank roof. Sometimes a weak spark would falter in its upward flight, waver as if undetermined where to go, only to find itself sucked onto the black roof planks to emit for a moment a surge of brilliance and become a part of the blackness.

"Oh-mee, my mother, why do the beautiful stars not all escape?" a small girl would ask.

I

THE SHORT ONE had volunteered to visit the master canoe builder who lived on the isle to the mouth of the sound. On his way there he had been granted a song. From the wind to the north a new song was born.

He began to sing it now above the brisk high-pitched sigh of the wind. He had a long way to go. There was plenty of time. The wind pushed him along. He was steering his canoe with his paddle and presently he began to tap and strike the gunnel as he measured the slow beat of his lyric. The whitecaps slapped louder, ever louder, to the flaring sides of his canoe. His song grew louder, bolder and strong. The song-maker had been granted a song.

YOO-AH-TI THE NORTH WIND

Whitecaps scudded merrily in the estuary
Yoo-ah-ti rejoiced and whispered a note
That was borne on the breath of the morn
From the heavens to the north it was born.

The note was faint but grew with the morn
Like the wind from the north it grew
And mellowed to a song that was new
Like whitecaps on the estuary.

The note came stealing through the wind
Sad, melancholy, alone for a time,
Growing, expanding, swelling through the mind
Settling to a song of Yoo-ee the wind.

The morning had broken clear and crisp. The river was calm. There had been no wind. That was good. A sign that Yoo-ah-ti, the North Wind, would come. It would die down again as the sun struggled to reach its zenith and dip to the west that seemed closer now. A perfect morning. A good time to put up the sail and follow the wind.

Peeping over the eastern hills the sun was climbing fast. It appeared round and sharp against wisps of fibrous clouds whose fingers reached up into the heavens only to dissolve again into the pale blue sky.

The sleek craft was easing itself out of the delta flats and suddenly shot into the stream of the ebbing tide. It was a beautiful canoe. On its high imposing prow a figure, Ah-tush the deer, was painted in vivid red against the char-black of the craft. A lone figure, he stood up and began to hoist a sail, as it eased up the slender mast its natural red-brown color mellowed out and shone warmly in the morning sun. Yoo-ah-ti, the North Wind, began to nudge the surface of the waters into ripples. The red sail billowed in the freshening breeze and the craft shot into the full stream of the down wind. The Short One resumed his seat in the stern.

Ah-tush — long, sleek, charcoal black against the rising sun sped merrily into the mainstream where frigid waters joined the warm sea-chuck, wavered, merged, dissolved itself momentarily into the morning mist at the estuary.

Slender clouds hung suspended midway up the western hillsides of the narrow inlet. They remained there, not moving one way or the other with the freshening breeze from the north. "Good. It is good. Yoo-ah-ti will remain for awhile."

The lone occupant of the craft was slim, lithe and short. It was because of his slight build that he was nicknamed The Short One. He had borrowed Ah-tush, the fast canoe, because it belonged to his elder brother who had built it himself. The Short One was not going down to see if the sealing canoe was finished. He was going mostly because the builder was also his brother and he wanted to sit awhile and listen to him talk, to hear about the coming event.

The Short One was the youngest brother from a large and influential House who long since had founded their own clan and moved into territory of their own. Now, at this time, one of his elder brothers was staging a Tloo-qwah-nah. The Short One was still very young and because of this he regarded the affair seriously indeed because even in his few years he had become a songmaker and dancer of high repute.

The Short One was still humming, inside of him were the notes that he had felt at the estuary, the notes falling together as the wind from the north increased with the morning, while wavelets spilled over whitecaps that drummed pleasantly at the flaring sides of his craft to gurgle, churn and effuse themselves back into the stream.

> Wind! Wind! Many. Multitudes. Like this be.
> Wind! Wind! Many. Multitudes. Like this be.
> Many. Multitudes. It is now, it is.
> Many multitudes will stay.
> Wind! Wind!

In accordance with the coast custom the uncle of the prospective host, on his mother's side, had taken all responsibilities into his able hands to see to the many requirements pertaining to the staging of a Tloo-qwah-nah play. Most of the smaller things had now been accounted for. There was the sealing craft that he had ordered some ten moons ago. The maker was reputed to be the best. He lived on an island a full day's journey if the north wind favored him with a good breeze that lasted most of the day. There was still one month to go ere the maker would come. One quiet night he would come and enter his lodge. He would sit and eat the evening meal beside the fire. When all things were done, news told and received, when the women retired and they were alone, when the host assured him that the robes were out and spread on the pallet for him to rest and spend the night he would rise and quietly say, "Oh,

I nearly forgot, your craft is done. It is ready. I will deliver it whenever you say."

To finish and deliver a sealing canoe was a gala event under normal circumstances but a Tloo-qwah-nah play was a bigger occasion. Accordingly, at such times, the builder waived all claims of courtesy, attention, ceremony and pomp. The purchaser quietly recompensed the builder in the privacy of his own fireside. The uncle was aware of this but nevertheless he was impatient. He must visit the builder, not so much to see if the craft had been finished but to sit and talk to the artisan.

He had resolved that the Tloo-qwah-nah would begin after Ghee-yah-kimlth, the Cutting Carving Moon, the moon that contained busy days, the all out fishing of most salmon species, of carving and cutting them into long thin strips, of placing with sure gentle hands the slender cedar sticks across the split salmon so that they would dry over the smoke. Of hunting the shy and timid hair-seals as they moved into their winter quarters at the heads of the long inlets away from the roar of the surf in the wintry gales of the outer isles. Of hunting and locating great schools of herring as they moved in from the sea, of catching them with long rakes at the dusk and also when the morning star twinkled down the far horizon to the west.

Tides were low at this time of the moons. It was the time to harvest clams, to gather the rich brown abalone from the shallows. The black mussels against the white foam of breakers invited the harvesters with their stout yew-wood hand spikes to come and peel them off the dripping rocks. It was the time when Hyish-toop, chiton, treasure crop of below normal low tides could be found clinging to rocks, when they showed themselves in great numbers and could be pried loose from the haven of wet and slippery rocks and thrown into kha-oots, baskets, that hung on tump-lines on the strong backs of the younger womenfolk and hauled directly to the lodges to be eaten raw or par-boiled over simmering coals.

Low tides made Tee-tloop, the octopus, an easy prey to the prodding spear of the hunter as he searched and poked under ledges beneath rocks in the shallows. When boiled over a fast glowing fire the meat was indeed a delicacy for aristocrats. It was white like the foam of Yoo-ah-ti, the wintery winds from the north upon the waters of an ebbing tide. Its red, red outer skin was peeled off and cast into the glow of dying embers.

The sea-cucumber, fat with sea water too, was within easy reach of the young men who revelled in choosing plump fire-brown cucumbers from shallow places and rolling them up with long poles. The women threw them into cedar baskets standing on wet sands above low water to carry to teams who were working on nearby rocks cutting the ends off, pulling the innards out and stringing them on cedar sticks ready to be dragged across sharp barnacles to scrape off the tough outer skin and tenderize them for cooking. The sea-cucumber was boiled slowly. Its casing was agreeably solid and contained a soft white substance that looked not unlike overcooked rice and tasted somewhat like macaroni. The low, low tides of the Cutting Carving Moon offered many more appetizing foods for the discriminating gourmets of the west coast.

Root experts were busy harvesting their own crops. The time had come to dig and bundle bracken roots, to poke in and twist sturdy stakes for the roots of Ah-ee-tso and Tleets-upe, plants that abounded along rocky beaches in the inlets. The leaves of Ah-ee-tso are cloverlike. Its meat is white, sweet and though not as solid as the carrot its taste is similar. The meat from the root of Tleets-upe is brown, thick and shaped like pretzels. Crunchy when eaten raw, it cooks into a pulp that tastes like bananas.

These roots were taken back to the village to be pounded and readied for the big roast or to be boiled rapidly to supplement the Qwah-niss that were already cured and stored away since early spring. Qwah-niss, the bulb of camas, was regarded by all Coast Indians as a special delicacy. Indeed, great feasts were given during Ah-yuh-kimtl, the Moon of the Great Spawn, March, when the first Qwah-niss were harvested by the matriarchs who owned and controlled large meadows and deltas where camas grew in profusion. Mhe-in, a bulb found growing sparsely amongst the camas, is also extremely sweet and palatable. The bulb is a rich brown and in most cases was eaten raw. The sea, the forest and the open land contained an abundance of food. The Indian said, "Let us share it with our fellow men."

The moon of the Cutting Carving season was drawing to a close. The more boisterous Cleansing Moon, November, would soon arrive. It was the Cleansing Moon that swelled the rivers and streams until they spilled water over their banks carrying the offal down to the sea. When the moon declined again the land was once more washed and cleaned with fresh sand to carpet the now barren beaches and protect the grass roots from pelting rain and chilling frost that would come with the Moon of Little Sister, December.

II

Choo, choo, choo, choo. Ready, finished, complete. Councillors, orators, artisans and heralds had sat together for the last time before the Tloo-qwah-nah. All was ready, all was waiting. Send out the urgent call, rush call, rush call. Send forth the rush call. The heralds stood up. We will go immediately.

The big canoe was waiting by the landing. There were six men there when the heralds arrived. The canoe was fully provisioned, ready to go. The half moon glowed dimly high in the heavens when the company departed from their home beach. There was no wind in the night. The air was still, sharp and crisp in the late autumn moon. The rains had come and gone again. The tide turned to ebb in the broad shallow stream. They would reach the first neighboring village when the morning star reached down to hide behind the western hill. The men paddled easily. There were no oars.

Yoooooo. Awake, awake! Hah-walth, Chah-chah-mah-dha, arise now and heed this call. This is to summon you to the great Tloo-qwah-nah. This is to bid you to come, hear the songs, see the dances and enjoy the plays. Hear now this hurry-up call. Here it is. The time has come. Bring with you your spouses, your sons, your daughters, your household. Hear now. You will come when the moon that has set behind your hills is spent and the new moon is restored to the western sky.

Hhh-ahh, Hah-walth, Chah-chah-mah-dha. That is all, O King, respective Chiefs.

The tide was out. The expanse of the beach was wet. Mist rose from the steaming sands. Blue smoke spiralled, floated low, drifted slowly to hang motionless in front of the great village. "Good weather will stay with us," mused the elder in the craft.

The great canoe stood at a respectful distance from the shore. This standing off position was in deference to the recognized owners of the landing strips or beaches, thereby removing the obligation for such owners to invite or receive any guests who might arrive at the landings.

However, in a short time three men from the village came down to the beach very quietly and as they drew nearer to the great canoe they beckoned the visitors to approach and land. When this was done the three men graciously invited the visitors to their respective lodges, going up quietly without any show of pomp whatsoever. There was no need for further ceremonies as these had been gone through during their first visit almost a year before.

This quiet hurry-up call was repeated in the other neighboring villages until all were invited. The emissaries returned home under cover of darkness again. The business of the Tloo-qwah-nah had begun. All things that needed to be done from then on must be performed in secrecy. Everything from now on must be done with the utmost gravity, solemnity and urgency. There was to be no more procrastination. All things must be done now and done promptly. All men and all women associated with the immediate House of the giver of this Tloo-qwah-nah must from now on and until the whole business was completed, give all his time and energy towards its success and grand culmination. This was the expected thing to do. This was the time when all ties of kinship were encouraged to grow, expand and extend beyond the mere security of relationship. This was the time when co-existence exemplified itself beyond the mere desire to be tolerant, to live and let live. This was the time to <u>share your good fortune, wealth and affluence with your fellow-man</u> be it your worldly belongings, your food or your goodwill. This was the time when <u>tribes of different dynasties were drawn together in one common bond — fellowship.</u>

Not all guests arrived on the same day. Accommodating and billeting them was not difficult. The huge lodges had ample room. Before long all guests were well taken care of, most of them being taken in by relatives.

It was natural for relatives to seek to land on beaches that belonged to their own kin. There was no delay or uncertainty in moving all guests indoors. By long continued practice the different factions fitted into their section of life. If there was any problem at all it was to curtail generosity towards the arriving guests. The results at these times were that all were wont to be overfed.

Often the king of each tribe would come in a flotilla of canoes. His own would be lashed to three or four of the largest to form a pontoon-like raft with wide boards secured to the top to form a large surface. This served well for any shows or dances that might be planned by the visitors. All the king's subordinates occupied this raft which was called Klooshingkuck.

While still at a distance the flotilla would strike up its own paddle song in complete unison with the stroke of their paddles. Singing louder and with more and more enthusiasm they drew nearer to the now waiting village until their song ended with a low receding note like the gushing waters of a cataract that had spent itself to fuse back into the sea. The momentum of the pontoon raft with all its paddles idle and motionless pulled it swiftly towards the sandy beach. There was complete silence. No words of welcome came from the host village. The great raft touched the white sand. Then an imposing figure, dressed in all his most glorious regalia, gave forth with a lusty rendition of his incantation especially reserved for an occasion such as this. The waiting owner of the stretch of sand hurried his special guests ashore and into his lodge.

On such occasions and in singular circumstances, as when the guest of honor was a king of a neighboring tribe or a chief of extraordinary repute and popularity, the host would place his array of singers propitiously along the sandy beach and in front of his great lodge in a semi-circle ready to offer their welcome song. The rest of the members stood in the background to accompany the singers with clapping of hands, beating of thunder-drums and banging of planks with rounded sticks. This was the Salute of Homage.

The expected guest would come, of course, with a lusty rendition of his own paddle song. As soon as the song ended the hosts would immediately strike up their welcome song, the leader standing in front of the singers with his eagle feathers held high above his head extolling the words or lyrics that were to be sung. As the first beat of the drum boomed forth, and simultaneously with the opening strains, twenty and four young braves stepped forth from the ranks each alternate one holding in his right hand a long slender pole with the end pointing straight up to denote, and to assure the visitors, that the manoeuvre was a friendly one. The braves deployed very deliberately towards the oncoming craft, keeping time with the drums as they slowly moved down the beach, then splitting their column as they reached the water. Both wings waded in to form an inverted wedge with an opening in the middle through which the craft glided. As its prow touched the sands the braves slowly closed in alongside the craft but keeping themselves at a respectful distance. Now they stood perfectly motionless at easy attention facing the great canoe. The occupants of the craft still held their paddles alongside and made no move, nor did they utter a word. The leader of the singers was once more extolling in a clear and vibrant voice the chorus of the song. "We bid you welcome." His gleaming feather baton was cleaving the air to accentuate and emphasize his intonation of the words of the chorus. "Come, enter my lodge. Share with me my wealth. With me partake of my oils, the fat, the abundance of my land."

Immediately, as the song leader commenced the intonation, the braves who flanked the canoe slowly and very deliberately slipped the poles to their waiting partners on the other side. As the song grew stronger and reached its highest pitch the great canoe was lifted slowly out of the water and heaved onto strong shoulders in one graceful movement. The welcome song came to a resounding end.

For a long moment there was no sound. No one moved. No one spoke. The water dripping from the raised canoe was loud and clear. Slowly, easily, with no hurry the chief occupant and object of this homage rose from his seat in the middle of the great craft, in his right hand he shook his rattle that he quavered in a steady continuous roll.

The man stood his full height. He was not tall but he was stocky with shoulders wide. Deliberately he raised the arm that shook the rattle until it reached the height of his own waist. He wore a magnificent robe of sea-otter. Around his small head he wore the traditional headdress, a band made from beaten bark of red cedar. The rich orange-red of new bark reflected the blaze of the morning sun. Save for the steady roll of the rattle there was no sound. The raised canoe heaved forward and began to move up the easy incline of the sandy beach. The throng above the landing made no move. There was no other sound. The roll lessened as the arm that held the rattle lowered again until it was straight down. The rattle remained horizontal. The roll was now almost inaudible. There was no hurry. The day was long.

Into the clear crisp air of the Moon of Little Sister, December, there issued a low faint undertone, a prelude to man's incantation. The roll of the rattle now increased as it

23

rose to the bearer's waist height once again. The voice trailed off and seemed to dissolve into the morning mist. The rattle rolled on. It was strong and vibrant now encouraged by the hand that held it parallel with the moving craft. The voice came back in a strong monotone. Except for the hand that shook the rattle imperceptibly the figure in the middle of the canoe borne aloft by stalwart braves remained motionless. There was no visible movement in the chanter's lips. Slowly, as if reluctant to escape the confines of the morning mist the voice increased in volume. The craft moved slowly. There was time. No need to hurry. The silence from the throng above the beach increased the tension that now prevailed in the entire atmosphere.

"Tloo-qwah-nah, I will do. It is said." The incantation had begun with utmost gravity. The voice was now strong, clear, resonant, escaping the confinement of the cold waters to soar into the morning air and cut deeply into the dense forest behind the great lodges.

"Tloo-qwah-nah. It is said. I will do." A high pitched voice issued from the waiting throng . . . or did it emanate from the tops of the tall pines that swayed ever so slightly with the morning breeze from the north?

A second rattle was heard from the direction of the throng.

"Kah-hahhhhhhhhhh." It was a female voice. Extremely high to begin with but gradually it subsided to a long-drawn-out note, terminating in a cadence of proud dignified intonation.

"Whykah-shee-tlahhh. Whykah-shee-tlah Nauhs." Halle-lu-jah to the Most High. Halle-lu-jah to the Most High.

The incantation, prayer song of the man in the canoe was being recognized. It was being honored. The prayer was supported by the entire tribe with the lone accompaniment of the female voice. The borne canoe moved up the sandy slope. The ceremony and procession reached the incline where the grass separated the beach from the upper level of the building

24

sites. The incantation trailed off into the distant hills, the lingering note receding lower and lower to an inarticulate, guttural and tremulous sound that seemed to return into the earth.

The bearers stopped their slow march. They lowered the canoe with all its occupants onto the sand. The solemn intonation from the lone female voice ceased. The rattles hung silent. There was no other response from the throng. The Indian prayer song was an orison. It was rendered not to man but unto the King, Creator of all living things; the Giver, Provider Of All Wants. Save for the Whykah-shee-tlahhh Nauhs, intoned most reverently, no one ever intruded, invaded or transgressed this sacred liberty.

Not all kings nor all chiefs received this honor. It was accorded only to the most influential and respected of the aristocracy. Indeed this ceremony was rarely seen. This recipient with his own sacred prayer song had silenced the throng. He was a man of honor.

Spread to the right of the craft there was a new cedar mat. It reached up the incline to the upper level and thence to the great doors of the lodge of the residing king. The honored chief stepped out onto this carpet and moved with measured steps to meet the usher who was moving down toward him. When the pair reached the upper level the remainder of the occupants of the craft rose from their seats and got out, taking particular care not to step onto the cedar mat. The company walked briskly in order to catch up with their chief before he reached the doors of the lodge and when they too gained the main grounds the throng moved slowly behind them towards the entrance. No sound was made after the ending of the dramatic rendition of the prayer song.

The great doors of the lodge were open and as the usher motioned the honored chief to enter there issued from the far end of the lodge a low introduction of the opening strains of a lively ditty. As the song leader completed the prelude he

25

motioned to the drummers who were placed conveniently to one side of the company of young women costumed in gay robes. They stood perfectly motionless along the width of the far end of the great open space within the lodge waiting to strike simultaneously with a resounding thump the battery of drums which boomed out a rich melodious impulse. The earthen floor, the low vaulted ceiling-roof of the great lodge and the divider partitions of cedar mats that hung on three sides of the crude theatre served well to subdue and restrain any harsh reverberation that might otherwise have occurred when the battery of twenty or so drums boomed forth their accompaniment. The singers sang lustily to encourage the troupe of young women of the village who now began to sway to and fro. Their arms outstretched at an easy angle and their hands held with palms turned upward to denote friendship, goodwill and acceptance to all guests who came with an open countenance and peace within their hearts.

As the tempo of singing and the boom of thunder-drums increased in volume so did the swaying of the wall of dancers until the whole column inclined first to one side then to the other, their arms always outstretched, swaying gracefully in a swinging motion, gesticulating always in outward and strewing motions to reassure the guests of complete welcome to share and partake of their affluence.

> The Power on high doth make me dance,
> The Power on high doth make my heart sing,
> The Power on high doth make me play
> The Power on high doth make me show my ritual.

The meaningful motions of the dancers executed so expressively, the exciting throb of the thunder-drums, the lilt, the increasing tempo and the song rendered so wholeheartedly dispelled doubt or suspicions. The song, the dance, in one grand sweep expressed eloquently the full meaning and the intent of a happy singing people.

26

The Power on high doth make me dance
Because wealth is in my house.
The Power on high doth make my heart sing
Because wealth, it is in my house.
The Power on high doth make me play
Because wealth, it is in my house.
The Power on high doth make me show my ritual
Because wealth, it is in my house.

The man in whose honor all this fanfare was displayed
showed no visible indication of surprise. He walked slowly.
There was no hurry. The day was long.

Led by the usher, he moved with his retinue that now fanned
out to both sides of him to the far side of the long lodge. The
crescendo of the Song of Gladness, the offering of goodwill by
the comely dancers which was still building up finally came
to its climax as the guest of honor reached the far end. The
song leader was now vigorously beating the air with his white
eagle feather baton. He held it high above his head, reaching
higher and higher until he was on tiptoe, stimulating, coaxing
and exhorting his singers to greater volume. The thunder-
drums increased in volume also with the singing — boomm-
boomm-boomm-boomm-boomm-boomm. The gesticulating
dancers offered with upturned palms the goodwill and giving;
with the casting off motions, the affluence of their land and
the abundance of their sea.

The wall of dancers shifted perceptibly so that an opening
in the centre occurred. The song leader slowly advanced towards his battery of drummers; he was now facing his drum
leader cleaving the air fervently and with gusto until with one
final downward sweep of his gleaming white feathers the
Song of Gladness ended abruptly. It ended with a resounding
boom of the thunder-drums and the strong tenor of the song
leader increasing the volume as he emphasized the last line.

Because, wealth, it is in my house.

The final boom of the drums, the melody of the song floated

upwards along the vaulted roof seeking escape and so wafted out of the smoke-hole at the highest peak of the lodge. There was silence. No one moved.

The dancers stood with heads bowed, their hands in front with fingers interlaced, denoting that their message had been delivered. The usher motioned towards the opening at the centre of the column of young women and the guest moved towards it and so entered, passing through to the inner room to be received by the residing king in his own chambers. The guest's young son and wife now followed closely while his retinue fell back and remained in the outer arena.

During the entire procedure of this grandiose show of pomp and singular deference the young man did not falter once, neither did he manifest or betray undue emotion. He reacted normally as if no special event was taking place. He moved slowly. There was time.

Other than his initial response with his own prayer song he made no further effort to answer, rejoin or rebut. This was ample evidence of his meticulous education and upbringing. The lord of the lodge was pleased with the young man.

The king of the domain where this Potlatch occurred was a kindly man with deepest eyes under long, luxuriant brows, swarty cheeks that shone, and a broad, expansive smile that showed a complete set of strong even teeth. He greeted the young man easily and showed no undue affectation when the usher announced the guest, his son and his tloots-ma, wife, in that order.

"Choo, choo, choo, Chah-mah-dah."

A standard and normal salutation of all west coast Indians that may be interpreted as, "All be well, Chief."

Immediately upon the entrance of the three guests the Hah-cumb, wife of the king, moved forward and warmly greeted the boy first in accordance with the teachings and belief that the child, particularly a son, took precedence over the mother. A mother was always welcomed, to be sure, but her offspring came first.

The ceremonial reception was the beginning of the formal opening that would commence the following day. The honored guest having been duly received and housed, all the other arriving guests were quickly and quietly taken care of. The order of the day was to make all guests comfortable.

"Hoooooooooo! Hoooooooooo!"

"Awake! Awake! Young men out of your couches. Awake, awake!" It was the village crier. His voice was clear, strong and commanding. "Awake and out with you! The sun will be up and out ere you know it. There is work to be done. Awake, awake, awake!"

It was the village crier's responsibility to rouse the villagers every morning and keep them posted of the time. He scolded and admonished the young men but none-the-less he was a popular member of the community. Moreover, it was he who called the assembly together with his penetrating commands of, "Walk you may now! Walk you may now!" that could be heard throughout the village.

The younger men of the village were expected to be at the chosen lodge for the great occasion well beforehand to prepare and carry out chores that must be done; to start the main fires, carry in wood, open the smoke-hole above each hearth, replenish drinking water and roll out the long cedar mats that served as rugs on the raised platform that encompassed three sides of the lodge where all guests were placed and seated. The great lodge was comfortably warmed with four fires blazing merrily.

From an early age children were encouraged and taught to be helpful. The senior member of any age group was considered to be the director of that operation and good-naturedly dubbed Huh-wilth, the King, because he was responsible for his entire group and their actions. As far as the young men were concerned he was the authority and they readily followed his instructions.

When the guests arrived all was in readiness.

III

Along the entire coast of Vancouver Island established areas were acknowledged to belong to tribes, with kings who exercised plenary authority over that area.

In many cases the areas included meadows for rootstocks, bulbs, berries and so on; hunting grounds for wild game; rivers and streams for salmon; shorelines for mollusks, crustaceans; shallows, reefs and shoals for rock fish and finally seaward areas bounded by established lines relative to and abiding by landmarks. Complete rights to these areas were sustained tenaciously and any infringement of hunting laws were severely dealt with. It was the law to take the first of any seasonal food to the residing king so that all members of his tribe might taste and partake of the food as it came in for the first time.

The council for a domain consisted of the chief and his subordinate chiefs. Influential seats in the council or senate were allotted to leaders according to their wisdom and abilities, men with proven wisdom, strength of character, and who were virtuous and impartial. It was these leaders who taught the masses and it was believed that good example did what any amount of admonition or set of secondary rules would not. Moreover, the strength and continuance of power depended greatly, if not entirely, on these qualities. Indeed, kings were known to disown an heir and revoke all pretensions, rights and claims that would normally have been his inheritance. However, this occurred only when such heir consistently showed weaknesses of morality or total rejection of inter-tribal laws.

Out of the council there emerged a tribunal to resolve and settle all disputes of consequence, oftimes including those of wars. From this council, too, came the ushers, whose business it was to know which particular seat belonged to whom; the advisers to the king; the mentors; the teachers; the story-tellers; the historian; and the orators who presented the message, articles of agreement and oftimes an ultimatum also.

An artist was sometimes inducted into the tight organization when and if he merited that honor because he was able to think profoundly and create forms with which to show the people and thereby to stimulate, encourage, provoke and win over to ideas and principles where mere words failed.

Moreover, inter-tribal consensus iterated that a tribe was the total image of its king and he was himself as strong as his council. Indeed the council possessed so much influence that it did, on isolated occasions, bear and compensate for the foibles and weaknesses of a timid, irresolute king. Howbeit, it was not long before that unhappy situation became common knowledge among other tribes. This would greatly jeopardize the king's position — so much so that influential tribes have been known to rapidly lose both power and position when the key figure in that senate was removed by death or other misfortune.

Thus a seat at the council and the right to occupy it was considered to be the highest award for the aspirant. Having once acquired a seat, and in order to continue, leaders guarded their offices with vigilance bordering on jealousy.

An usher's training began very early in his life. It was absolutely necessary for him to know each House and each family's background and history so that he might place them according to their social standing when they arrived at gatherings and feasts. Like all other training his lessons began by

32

his being present with his father or uncle, as the case might be, in social gatherings. By the time he became a full-grown man and because of his prolonged association with the actual procedures he became proficient and was then in line to become the next assistant usher and so on up the social ladder until he reached his goal as head usher.

This restricted control of policies by the ruling class did create distinct stratas of social orders but it also prevented ambitious, conniving pretenders from usurping power from recognized rulers. Though succeeding rulers were hereditary, if an heir was known to be morally weak the sire's nephew, his eldest sister's son, took precedence over his own sons. Unhappy situations such as this did occur but they were relatively isolated. The good of the tribe was considered above the rights of heirs.

When the guests began to arrive for the Tloo-qwah-nah each household came in a body, the head member entering first, followed by his eldest son, then the rest of the members with the mother entering last. If, however, the mother was the head of her house, she preceded all others.

Each head man's name was announced in a clear ringing voice by the usher and his assistant conducted the head to his seat while his family was directed to a nearby area reserved for them.

The ruler occupied the head seat, his heir next and so on down the social register, the lesser seats receding towards the doors.

THE SPEAKER

Choo Why, Choo Why.   Hear ye, hear ye.
Rulers, chieftains, queens, revered young ones,
Braves, clansmen, commonalities, all.
Listen you now, for the voice of this House,
Whose seats you have graced with your person.
It will utter, yea, with many voices will it utter.

33

Thanks, many thanks are due you for your person;
For the presence of your own, here in mine.
When my voice sallied forth to your domain
You responded, with your House you came,
Into my lodge you entered, now it is complete.
For this my heart is full with joy, replete.

You enter my lodge, not as strangers
Tribes from far and near, great and small
With awakened conscience, know that your clan
By the blood of ancestors of yore
Belong also to this House, that is ours.
Let it be.   Let it stand, secure the ties that bind.

The time is come again, it is here with us this day.
On the wings of the crescent it is borne;
On the growing Moon of Little Sister, it is come
Once again to bid us all: Renew the ties that bind.
The urge to tell traditions old is here again.
To hear again from whence our bonds began.

Forebears of yours and mine of long ago
By union of wedlock, were joined as one.
Their offspring remain with you and with me.
Tenets you have instilled into your young
Move hand in hand with my own.
Thus your House and mine are as one.

Let us this day, clasp our hands again
Like our forebears who made the bond.
Let us recall, traditions that are old
Like our ancestors did of long ago.
Let us, this day, open our hearts again
Like our sires did with songs so bold.

Sing now with me, the songs you know
Let your voices grow strong with mine.
Lift the foundations of my lodge now
When you join mine with your own.
Heed the throb of thunder-drum, that is mine;
Arise and clap your hands in time.

Play with me the games you know so well.
Dispel all fears to the wind from the north.
Stand now and laugh with my House.
Display your knowledge of my To-pah-ti*
The games of skill, of strength and for the mind
My conscience is good, it swells with pride.

Hear again the stories that are old;
Traditions that our ancestors told.
The laws they made are still with us
They are here and are still with us
They are here and have not changed.
Our lands, our streams, our seas remain
To provide for wants, that are yours and mine.

See again my dance of joy and gladness.
Cast your woes to the winds from the north.
Stand with me and share my happiness;
Take my hand, with me stand forth.
Do the dance your forebears and also mine
Did leave for us to perform as one.

Thanks, many thanks are due you for your own.
The presence of your House here in mine
Reassures that friend is nigh.
Arise, renew the friendship of all time
Show the goodwill to all mankind
Share with me the abundance of our seas.

Uhh-aye.   Uhh-aye.   Rest ye.   Rest ye.
Rulers, chieftains, queens, revered young ones
Braves, clansmen, commonalities, all
Comfort now your limbs for the while.
Hark!   Now the voice of this House will come
Yea, with many voices will it come.

*Mystical inherited rites.

35

IV

THE SPEAKER FOR THE House stood a little to one side of the
residing king. In his left hand he held the Talking Staff. He
held the stick to display the ornate carvings that adorned the
top portion that represented his office and indeed was the
official symbol for the speaker of the tribe. His voice was low
yet penetrated to the farthest corner of the great lodge with
its earthen floor and vaulted roof. He spoke slowly, with ease,
without effort, he hurried not. No need for haste. There was
time. The day was long.

His voice was soft like the sigh of the wind from the north.
It would change with no effort, like the sound of waters that
run in the rapids, to soar into the heavens, to be heard in the
vale beyond the pines that screen the hills. He spoke like the
waves on the sands of a summer's eve, low and calm, yet
stealing through the wood, penetrating the bole, to be heard
in the glen beyond the canopy of salal. Oftimes it whispered
like the breeze from the south that coaxed the wavelets to
scud yet a little farther up the beach on a rising tide.

His voice was quiet and ran deep, like the pool below the
waterfall. Gently it came, like the tide from the sea, and
penetrated deep within your heart. It stilled all fears and
soothed the conscience, it called, coaxed, encouraged, stimulated and inspired old and young to sense, to feel, to want
the simple joy that comes from the honest fellowship of mankind.

Unspeaking sat the throng in the lodge with the earthen floors. Little children huddled closer to their mothers, little boys climbed to fathers' knees, older boys edged closer to uncles, but not because of fear or apprehension.

The speaker had reached his audience. He had surmounted the normal and ever present doubts and skepticisms that haunt all mankind. True, the young did not comprehend the meaning of the formal address, nevertheless, they were all completely captivated by the open and winning personality of the speaker. He spoke to them as well as to his adult audience and the young felt very much a part of the vast throng.

Like all positions of importance the speaker had acquired his from his father who preceded him. His uncle had taught and coached him with great patience. There had been many hours of sitting at the tops of distant hills and mountains when the breath from the north caressed the crown of the pine and wisps of white clouds were wont to expand into space, to reach farther out to the brow of the horizon; of admiration of Kup-chah, the voice of the rapids, that rises to the heavens and vaults over the hills; of visits to the seashore on a summer's evening when the tide was coming in, and feeling the lap of the small waves upon the strand to be heard beyond the bole of the mighty spruce and so into the dense forest; of watching the summer wavelets being coaxed to reach farther up the beach with the rising tide; of sensing, feeling the soothing effects of the quietness of the pool below the waterfall and perceiving the divine hand as well as the fantasies borne on an incoming tide. The rise and fall, the inflection of the speaker's voice, his air, his mien, the look on his face, bespoke all these and more.

The speaker's voice flowed on slowly. He said many things to the fathers and to the mothers, he reminded them of their responsibilities to their young; he addressed the younger men and women as the revered ones and praised them eloquently for their willing participation in all the events.

Choo why tligh. Hear ye once more.
To the boy, to the girl, the revered ones
Thanks, many thanks are due you also
For your presence in this House
Here with this gathering in this lodge
Because of this you strengthen this House that is ours.

Stay close to your father, mother,
Your aunt, uncle and your Nah-neek-soo*
The tenets they impart are good for you too
The love that they show is all for you.
Let it be. Let it stand. Do not change
It gladdens the heart of those who stand for you.

These were not his own words. It was his duty to arrange, to say, to remind and to impart to the young, in words they would understand, the desire to be part of the gala event that they sensed was coming. Thus they became truly involved by watching and by being there listening to the teaching and, in fact, reviewing, affirming and declaring regulations governing the participation of children in all gatherings, particularly the Tloo-qwah-nah, in a manner that would most likely reach their age group.

It was evident that he had accomplished his intentions. No one stirred; no one moved from his allotted seat; all eyes were on the speaker to hear, to gather and grasp the meaning of his words. There was no hint of command. There was instead a hint of plea, entreaty, a suit imparted to those who wished to listen. It was evident the speaker had reached the heights few orators could aspire to.

Involve, include, submit yourselves
On the morrow or when the time arrives.
For your safety trust your elders.
No harm will come to you, be sure.
The time is come, it is here now,
To play, be merry, put all cares away.

*Grand-parent.

The time is come for you to join
To become a part of the whole.
This House will not, cannot, grow to flower
Without the buds, the shoot, the sprout
That sprang from the core that is our own.
Rest secure, submit yourselves on the morrow.

He spoke at length. He said many things more. Though
his words were directed to the young at this time, his intentions
included that of reminding the parents and the elders of their
immediate obligations towards their own children and wards
who were to be admitted into the secret society of the Tloo-
qwah-nahs.

The numbers were known beforehand and all the arrange-
ments were made. Guardians and parents had submitted fees
of food, utensils or hunting equipment to augment the store
and fund that would pay the costs of the gala event. There was
no set fee. Each participant paid according to his ability.
Indeed some children were admitted "in addition to" another
child. This was an exclusive society in that all aspirants were
required to believe and practice the tenet of sharing all foods
and the opulence of land and sea. This was the law of the
people of the land.

Choo why Tligh, Hoo-Ahs.   Hear ye, again, once more;
Chah-ma-dah;   always, it is the custom for all time
To put to the end that which is good.
Good you are;   a young man, alive, gracious, kind
    and generous.
Good judgment you have shown, throughout your
    growing years.
Thanks, many thanks are due your person.

The tenets of ancestors, you have taken,
To good use you have made our creed.
The laws, you have followed, unshaken.
To your people, you have shown great deeds.
Let it be;   let it stand, wax stronger more;
To the young impart strength, hope and honor.

It is not for man to repay
For the standards you have shown.
It is not for man to say, "I give."
Just reward that is yours will come
When man will call your name and say,
"Help!   Come nigh to me.   I am in need."

We hail, we lift you on to our land
With all respect at our command.
At this time, this is all that we can do.
We voice the joy that is in our mind.
At this time, this is all that we can say,
Thanks, many thanks are due your person.

Purposely the speaker had left to the very end of his address the tribe's final acknowledgement to the young chief's attainments as a paragon for the younger generation of all the tribes along the coast. In addition to the many virtues he had manifested the young man had harpooned and captured his first whale and had given a great feast in his own home for his House. He was blessed with a good life-mate and a young son four winters old.

The first response made to the address was the House from which the hero of the great gathering came. Its speaker was a kindly man with a brilliant command of language which he expressed to the best advantage. He acknowledged without hesitation the role of their host. He reaffirmed the inseparable union of the two tribes by virtue of blood wrought by ancestors of long standing. Graciously he gave thanks for the great honor conferred upon their own young chief and for the acknowledgement of virtues that all men aspire to. He assured their host of continued allegiance. His would strengthen the bond. He said more. With utmost skill, adroitness, wisdom and feeling the speaker intimated to all fellow guests the true intent of all feasts, particularly the Tloo-qwah-nah, which was the renewal of friendship, fellowship, partnership and good service to all mankind.

Nine other speakers stood, each with his mace of office.

Each reiterated words already said. Each swore allegiance to the ten tribes present in the great lodge with the earthen floors and vaulted roof.

When the address and the last response was heard the dusk of evening of the first day was stealing and creeping on silent wings upon the great lodge. The four fires that gave light and warmth were low for want of fuel. There were no windows to let in light from the sun. A lull came in the whole affair. There seemed to be a marked break, an expectation in the darkening atmosphere. Blue smoke from dull sluggish fires spiralled upward in search of an opening through which to escape the gloom and vanish into the remaining daylight.

Khootch-hh khootch-hh khootch-hh!

Without warning the crack and cackle of the raven's call rent asunder the silence.

"Whoy! Whoy!" The warning cry of awesome fear issued from the inner section of the host's quarters.

"Whoy! Whoy! Hark! Take heed. Listen now to the raven's voice. He brings tiding, this we know."

Little children hid small faces in their mothers' breasts, small boys climbed closer on their fathers' laps while the older boys sought the sturdy haven of their uncles' arms. No response. No one moved. No one spoke.

Khootch-hh khootch-hh khootch-hh!

The rasping call was nearer now. It seemed to be inside — and yet did not. Four times the nerve-shattering call sounded. Once at each corner of the lodge with the earthen floors.

Khootch-hh khootch-hh khootch-hh!

"Tidings, tidings, tidings. The raven brings tidings. Hark, ye! The raven journeys to all places. The raven sees all things. The raven smells all things. He knows all that comes to pass. Listen now and take heed of the message he brings to us all."

Khootch-hh khootch-hh khootch-hh!

There was silence. Not even a whimper from a child. Blue smoke spiralled upwards from dying fires.

41

Bang! Bang! Bang! Bang!

Into the dead silence smote four paralyzing, ghostly knocks upon the back wall of the great lodge. Like angry bolts of thunder that were too near, the nerve-shattering knocks sundered the silence that may have stayed or lingered too long. Four times the dreadful knocks came. Four loud knocks upon the dry cedar walls of the four sides of the lodge.

Bang! Bang! Bang! Bang!

The foreboding demanding challenge for entry boomed inwards and echoed around the great open room, for all the cedar mats that normally hung to separate family quarters had been removed. No cots. No robes for bedding. Nothing could be seen around the great lodge except the wide dry cedar-plank walls.

A small group of young men had eased their way towards the four fires that were dying for want of fuel upon their hearts.

Each group huddled closer to the fires seeking warmth.
Casting eerie shadows across the earth floors.
Blue smoke spiralled upwards in search of escape from
the gloom.

Presumably the same man who had given the loud warning cry of Whoy! Whoy! now moved forward slowly, and apparently with great fear. His step faltered, stopped, uncertain where to go. He was a frail man and looked very old. In his left hand he carried a crooked black cane. When he paused to turn back uncertainly he espied the knot of young men huddled around the smoking fire that offered no light and no warmth and seemed to take heart for he turned towards them and in a clear and harsh voice admonished them for their shamefulness.

"Young men never go near fire. Never stand near fire to warm your backs. Never stand around idle. Make yourselves useful; get some wood and pile it on that dying fire."

This outburst, especially from an elder, was unusual indeed.

It added more fear to an already tense situation. Silence gripped harder with cold, empty, depressing, morbid apprehension of the unknown. All exits and doors were bolted tight. The air in the great lodge was stifling, blue smoke from the dying fires faltered visibly and did not rise but instead sought escape into the already ghostly atmosphere. There it hung, undecided where to go.

Squeak. Squeak. Squeak. Squeak. Screech. Screech. Screech. Screech. Squall. Squall. Squall. Squall. Squeak-screech, squall-snarl-yarr-growl-yawp-whinyyyyy-oooooooo.

There was the loudest ear-splitting, nerve-shattering din that crash-shattered the silence, that had lingered and stayed too long. In quick succession the awful noise sounded four long-drawn-out times. It went around the lodge knocking and thumping on the four walls.

"Young men, throw some logs on that dying fire!" Now it was a direct command. The old man's voice cracked with desperation.

"Throw some logs on that fire!" he repeated. "We are being invaded! Qwha-yha-tseek, the timber wolf, invades our lodge."

A faint faltering roll of the rattle sounded from the women's section, grew stronger. Presently a figure appeared from the gloom. The blue smoke hung motionless in the air. The figure made her way gingerly to the front.

As she raised her arm that held the rattle the roll increased in volume only to die out completely. There was complete silence. No one moved. No one spoke or uttered any sound to help her in her brave effort to ward off or invade the awful silence.

Then seemingly with great effort, she raised her arm again and the rattle rolled once more. It was noticeably stronger this time. Slowly and deliberately she raised her head until she was looking straight ahead and there issued, as from nowhere, a high plaintive note. It seemed to come from a very great distance.

43

The doleful note gradually descended until it seemed to enter the lodge, pervading, permeating the still, silent place. The roll of the rattle sounded forth with renewed vigor and the note settled down into an entreaty, an incantation, a prayer song.

The young men around the dying fires, jolted out of their lethargy, piled great cedar logs feverishly onto the dying fires, spilling bags of whale oil, refined for that specific purpose, into the midst of the piled logs and into the live embers. This caused an immediate burst of towering sheets of flame that licked their sinuous and violent ascent up to explode through the narrow aperture of the smoke-hole atop the vaulted roof, sucking up with it the blue smoke and the pall, leaving a glaring light and waves of heat that could be felt throughout the great lodge.

There was light, an abundance of light. There was warmth. The voice, the petition, the invocation swelled with the gathering light in the great open area that had been so utterly foreboding with the gloom of the dying fires.

> Tloo-qwah-nah, I will do.
> It is said by The Power.
> Hark! I do hear, I understand.
> I will do the Tloo-qwah-nah.

The chant hurried not. Four times it repeated the verse. There was time. No need for haste. The night was long.

Logs blazed, the wild fire crackled and burst great sparks upwards through the open smoke-hole and so out into the gathering gloom of eventide. At last the incantation ended and silence once more prevailed except for the many voices from the fire.

Yawl-Ho-oooooooooooooooo

> Choo Why Tligh!   Choo why Tligh!
> Qwha-yha-tseek, the Wolf clan, it is their voice.
> The tidings have come, it is with us now.

Understand the message;   we must now play.
Show now, your thunder-drum, take it with pride '
The time has come to sing our many songs.

Yawl-Ho-oooooooooooooooo

The answering howl of the timber wolf sounded very near, to be followed immediately by a chorus of blood-curdling howls from all sides of the great lodge. Four times the voice of the Wolf clan sounded. The last call came from far, far away. The plaintive chilling sound died into the distance.

The doors of the lodge opened and a great rush of fresh air entered the now brightly lit lodge. The spell was broken. The suspense ended. The clan from Wolf land had been repelled. A great bonfire was made in front of the lodge, sending forth big sparks into the still air.

During the entire ordeal of the drama and suspense there was no apparent terror displayed from any of the numerous small children. The physical presence of mother, father and uncle was enough to allay all fears of the harsh, disturbing and frightening noises and sounds they had heard. This was good. This was ample evidence that the children had complete faith and trust in their parents and guardians. There was indeed complete understanding and communication between child and parent, however unconscious it may have been. The old man with the black cane was deeply aware of this and he was thankful. He beamed visibly and stood straighter and taller as he lingered to survey the throng as they filed out of the lodge.

V

Hoooooooooooooooooooooo!

Walk now, at once!   Walk now, at once!

Hoooooooooooooooooooooo!

Walk now, at once!   Walk now, at once!
There it be, the morning star.
The day will open, to'ards the east.

It was the familiar voice of the village herald, calling,
urging the people to make haste to the lodge.

Let not the king, the chief in his lodge, sit alone
The fire is lit in the lodge, burns brightly for everyone.
Let no man wait for your arrival.
The thunder-drum is warmed, take it now with pride.
Walk now, at once!   Walk now, at once!
Let not the king, the chief in his lodge, sit alone.

The morning air of the second day was chilly. Cold mist
rose from the calm surface of the river nearby, rising upwards
slowly in wide gray ribbons, pulling all things into wavy weird
shapes.

Long before the new day opened towards the east the young
men who were assigned to that purpose for the duration of the
entire Tloo-qwah-nah had rekindled the fires. All four blazed
merrily with no smoke visible and with only an occasional
spark that escaped the updraft pull of the fires. The great
doors were open; the air indoors smelled fresh and clean.
Serenity and contentment prevailed.

46

Light towards the east was growing stronger now. Dawn was opening a new day in a quiet way. The arête of the mountain loomed sharply against the awakening dawn. Light fleecy clouds with long tapering fingers reached upward into the still atmosphere. White flames danced against the now starless sky.

The last of the guests had arrived. There was a low hum that hung motionless over the entire inside area; it neither rose nor subsided, disturbing no one.

Choo-why choo-why.
Here we are again, this newborn day.
We know now what it is to be.
Comfort your limbs and settle down.
It is the queen who opens the play.

It was the old man with the black cane speaking again. There was a pronounced lilt to his voice, the worried look of morbid premonition of yesterday was not there. As he spoke he turned slowly to his left so that his voice could be heard at all corners of the great lodge. He emphasized his message which was short with up and down motions that kept perfect time with the tapping of his cane on the earthern floor. He showed no care, he beamed with confidence.

A well-modulated voice issued from behind the screen that separated the chief's quarters from the rest of the lodge. It was the introductory lines or bars of the song that was to be used in the actual opening of the Tloo-qwah-nah.

Presently the singer appeared from an opening. His back was turned towards the open arena and he approached backwards, beating time with the traditional eagle feather fan-shaped baton which he held high in the air. Next appeared the drummers. They too came out with their backs towards the audience. When the fourth and last drummer made his appearance the song leader moved to the left of the open area, manoeuvering his drummers so that they faced the people while he directed them with his gleaming white feathers.

The first of the dancers appeared, very slowly and very

47

deliberately approaching the arena. The second, the third, all came in with their backs towards the people, now the fourth came out. Each held her hands out in front with palms turned upwards, moving to and fro in a throwing, strewing motion. First to the right, then to the left they threw, keeping time with the drums. At a given beat all four turned in one graceful movement to face the audience, one two, one two, the beat grew stronger as more and more dancers appeared until the entire arena was encircled with a continuous line. The same movements continued throughout; first to the right, then to the left, the sweeping half-turn an exaggerated swoosh and flurry, their outstretched hands almost touching the floor.

This was the same troupe of young women who welcome-danced the young chief as he entered from the historic canoe lift the previous day only this time there were a great many more girls. It was the Chief's Dance executed by his wife and her own special troupe of dancers.

They wore long shawl-like robes whose edges reached the floor. When the troupe moved to and fro with the half-turn the whole column swayed and undulated so that the two-tone sound was like steady movements over a stand of rushes on an early summer's morn when the gentle wind from the north caresses with hands that cannot be seen by mortal man. Around their heads and their wrists there were tied the young shoots of hemlock, twisted to make tiaras of evergreen, symbolic of all nature, of goodness and the continual growth engendered by the Provider of All Wants.

Here I am. I offer my services. I share with you the opulence of my land and sea. Accept my goodwill to you and to your revered ones. To the east, the north, the west and the south, to the four corners of the wind I offer the joy that is in my heart this day.

This was the message of the movements and dance as presented by the young women of the tribe.

The Tloo-qwah-nah Play was opened by the women of the

48

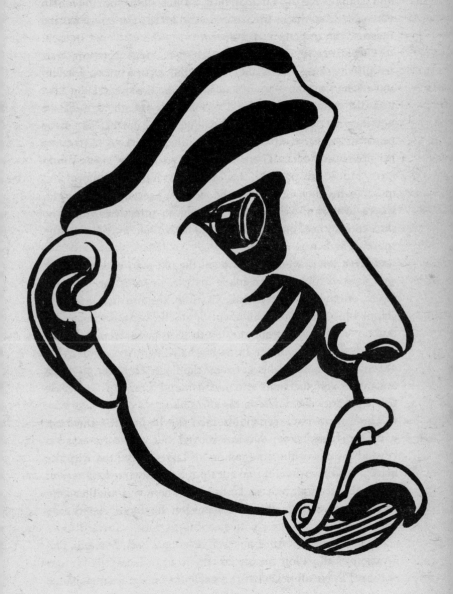

Mask of Plenty

tribe because the female represented the utmost grace, beauty and compassion of all mankind. A girl or a young woman was called, us-ma, which means the loved, the precious, the revered, the undefiled, the chaste.

The Dance of Greatness and Opulence had just come to a resounding finale with the last of the troupe moving backstage when a young man staggered into the great lodge. He was dishevelled, panting and gasping for breath as he stood not far from the entrance, unwilling to go farther in; great beads of sweat stood out on his forehead and trickled down his tired, tired face. There was fear and dismay in his young face. He stood panting, his shoulders hunching more and more in his dejection. Thus he stood, uncertain what to do, where to go and what to say. Slowly, in utter frustration, he sank to his knees on the earthen floor. No one moved. No one spoke. There was no help.

After a long, agonizing moment the old man with the black cane moved forward and made his way towards the prostrate figure on the floor. He took his time because fear had also gripped his heart. For a moment he stood over the young man but no word came from the figure with sweat gleaming like oil and spreading down from his hair-line. At long last the old man also sank to his knees on the floor. He must go down and approach the man and not demand from up above. So the old man went down on his knees also.

The young man raised his face slowly towards the man with the black cane; his lips moved but no word escaped beyond the ear of the old man on his knees. Presently, with the help of his cane the old one got up reluctantly, crossed over to where the king sat and spoke to him. There was another long pause, then with forthright submission he faced the throng and in a voice wrought with fear blurted out, with a distinct catch in his voice, "All is not well. We have been entered. The invasion of the Wolf people last night was successful. We did not repel as we all believed. It is evident that our own vigilance for the unexpected had relaxed. This is bad, bad, bad.

He straightened himself as well as he could against the terrific strain that he was visibly laboring under, brought the tip of his black cane down on the packed earth floor of the lodge and called out a name, a second name, a third and a fourth; he went on calling out names until there were ten. There was no answer. No one spoke. No one moved. There was no help.

The old man with the black cane put his head down once again, his thin shoulders slumped down with it. He was staring at the earthen floor and his weak voice came again.

"The children of these names are gone. They are not with us. They have been abducted by the Wolf People." His voice trembled, the last words rasped out in dismay and utter defeat. "Not here. Not here."

WHOOOOOOOOOOOOOoooooooooooooo . . . .

It was the call of the wolf again. There was no hint of plaintiveness or mourning but a distinct indication of triumph, conquest and victory in the call. The throng hastened out in time to see the wolves make their appearance from across the clearing on the far side of the river. There were, in all, ten wolves slinking in and out of the reeds in the early morning fog and the mist from the river.

WHOOOOOOOOOOooooooooo . . . . Four times the call sounded.

"The fire; make the fire young men! Where are the young men? Logs, logs, pile on the logs, make the fire!"

The old man with the black cane became remarkably alert after his ordeal indoors. Young men piled on cedar logs and before long there was a roaring fire blazing with huge yellow-orange flames rising. The elders stood to one side of the knot of people watching intently every movement of the pack of wolves. In the early hours of the misty morning they looked so real but howbeit a loud boooooo was heard from the, thus far, staid elders.

Immediately an especially large and ferociously ardent wolf disappeared behind a screen of tall reeds and so back into the nearby woods. The remaining wolves lingered and moved with stealth, weaving furtively with the early morning mist. When at last all the wolves merged into the reeds and no more could be seen the old man with the black cane came forward, calling for attention.

"Hark, hark! I hear voices. Listen!"

"Mother! Come and get me." From behind the thickets up the hill the plaintive voice came.

"Mother, come and get me."

"Whoy, whoy. It is her voice, it is her voice. I know that voice. It is the child. It is the child."

Then other voices were heard over and above the hissing of the great fire in front of the lodge with earthen floors and vaulted roof, all calling their parents, their uncles in pleading small voices. "Come and get me."

"The Wolf People have our children captive. Go home, all of you go home! Stay there! Do not come out! We will sit and plot out the wisest course to pursue. We will get our children back safely."

The top men in the king's senate had been duly summoned into the inner chamber of the lodge with earthen floors and vaulted roof. They had sat behind closed doors. No one was permitted inside the lodge, no man, no woman, no child, none. All day, throughout the night the wise men sat; the evening and the morning star had come and gone again.

Mist on the river had lifted, the early morning fog that blanketed the low lying valley diffused upwards, revealing the faint blue of sky. The little patch of green across the river looked serene, the reeds and rushes in their proper place, denying evidence of any visit by man or beast. The fires both indoors and out were again dying out for want of wood. Quiet. Quiet. Quiet. No one was astir.

Hooooooooooooooooo!
Hooooooooooooooooo!

Walk, now at once!   Walk, now at once!
Let not the king in his lodge sit alone.
Walk, now at once!   Walk, now at once!

Hooooooooooooooooo!
Hooooooooooooooooo!

Young men moved about at the front of the great lodge
where the fire was lit, piling cedar logs on to it again and long
sheets of orange-red flame could be seen licking upward in
the still air as the whale oil was poured on to the live embers, sending out great sparks in every direction, creating loud
crackling sounds. The people responded. In long files, they
came ambling, moving slowly to the area around the now
roaring fire.

The old man with the black cane came out of the lodge.
He moved slowly and apparently with no care in the world;
he strode over to a man who was warming his drum near the
fire, whereupon more drums appeared, to be warmed also.
The rest of the councillors remained indoors or showed no
particular interest or care regarding the capture of the children.

It was assumed that the people coming out from their homes
now at this precise moment did not know, were unaware of
the dire circumstances at hand; that ten of their loved and
revered ones were missing and were in the hands of the Wolf
People. The natural course of the day was then to carry on as
if nothing had happened. This was called Wick-ee-chitl, know
nothing.

"We shall sing. Take hold now your thunder-drums and
lift your voices so that they echo and re-echo from the wall
of forest on the hill." The old man spoke easily. No need for
haste. There was time. The day was long.

A song started with a few men and women but soon the
numbers increased as one song ended and another began until

the entire throng that had congregated in front of the lodge, where the fire roared and great sparks burst out in every direction, joined and became a part of the great sing-song. Women detached themselves and formed a half-circle next to the cedar plank sides of the lodge and started the Dance of Gladness, swaying this way and that way. This sing-song went on for many hours, well on into the late half of the day.

In the late afternoon mist returned to the surface of the river, stealing towards its banks and to the patch of green where the reeds and the rushes stood, now with effort hoping to see the Moon of Little Sister grow to its full round of light up there in the sky. The fire that had reached up so high with its live sheet of flames waned again for want of fuel because the young men were busy with their drums for the singers and the dancers.

WHOOOOOOOOOOOOOOOO . . . .

That dreaded wolf call again! From across the river it came, from deep within the woods the call came and in a surprisingly short time the answering call came. It sounded very close. Before the company of singers and women dancers could go indoors for protection the first wolf appeared on the patch of green across the river, the second and the third appeared in quick succession until ten of them were on the green. They lingered, stealing in and out of the stand of reeds, unwilling to leave in spite of the fire that the people again rekindled with great haste to ward off another invasion or attack. After their fourth call and appearance the wolves slunk back into the thick woods across the river. There was no further sound save for the crackling of the great sparks from the fire.

"Indoors. Indoors! Get inside, we must now be vigilant!" It was the old man with the black cane again.

The singers, the dancers, the people went indoors reluctantly for no doubt they felt safe enough outside with the great fire again roaring and hissing in front of the lodge.

54

Once inside with the great doors closed tight the singing resumed, one song after another, light ballads and songs with no special significance to the crisis at hand, no sacred chants, no invocations were chanted but the singing continued without interruption, one song after another. The beat of the thunder-drums never ceased — oomb, oomb, oomb, oomb.

There was no special song leader any more. Men and women alike offered their own ballad as the previous singer finished his. This was the Wick-ee-chitl, the know nothing. The people knew nothing — only happiness.

The Moon of Little Sister was waxing strong and fast with the mystery of silent growth, reluctant now to retire out of sight in the early evening when there was so much to see down there on the banks of the river called Tsoh-mah-uss, but she must go because the stars in the sky must come out too and take their turn in shedding light to man and beast with their glow and twinkle as they danced across the Milky Way.

Great sparks burst out of the narrow smoke-holes on the ridge of the great lodge with earthen floors and vaulted roof, climbing straight up and up until the early night air swallowed the lurid flowing stream of red — or perhaps it journeyed up to mingle with the stars along the Milky Way. This marked the fourth day since the ten children disappeared — perhaps, perhaps taken by the Wolf People.

There was a temporary lull in the singing from inside the lodge, perhaps some more cedar logs were being piled on, or perhaps the womenfolk were lining up for another dance, but the sound of thunder-drums continued on and on . . . oomb, oomb, oomb, oomb . . . never ceasing, never missing a beat. Not loud, no boom, but the sound penetrated into the night air through the thick cedar planks of the walls and up through the smoke-hole to escape with the stream of living warmth of the sparks, to vault the stand of spruce that made the wall, to be heard and felt beyond its barrier and so into the depths of the dense forest . . . oomb, oomb, oomb, oomb. . . .

Suddenly there was a terrible commotion in the front. The great doors slowly swung open and into the twinkling light of the fire a tall man appeared. He was decked with the green of spruce. Around his head, his waist, his wrists and ankles was tied the prickly green of the spruce tree. It was believed that the prickles of spruce would ward off all evil so it was readily assumed that the man had been to or near a place fraught with danger. Perhaps he had been to the land of the Wolf People. Perhaps?

The figure held his ceremonial rattle in his hand. Very slowly he advanced and as a second figure entered he raised his hand which held the sacred rattle. Its faint roll was barely discernible above the sound of the <u>drums</u>. Presently his voice boomed forth above all other sounds, silencing the singing and the drums completely.

> Down to the mountain tops, he descends, Tootootch.
> It is he, with his help, his guidance and forceful meaning
> That I gather strength to do the Tloo-qwah-nah;
> Down to the mountain tops he descends, Tootootch,
> Sent down to me from He Who Provides All Wants.
> With strength in my heart, I do the Tloo-qwah-nah.

His voice was strong, imbued with the sureness of power. There was no hint or suggestion of doubt or timidity; there was instead distinct implication of courageous deeds, past and still to come. With utmost conviction did he render his orison which gave thanks, more than it asked, for acts yet to come.

The second figure was now inside the area of light flickering from the bursting, sparking fire. He too was decked with the green of spruce. To his right he escorted a small girl, daughter of one of the lesser chiefs, she was adorned with the green of hemlock. Following the child was her mother who, likewise, was adorned with the green of hemlock. She advanced into the arc of light with ritual solemnity, her right hand held high as she moved forward, her right foot leading to take a long slow step to push her whole body forward, only to pull back again before she continued for the next step. With her right arm held at a prayerful attitude she made these movements four times without change or variation, then on the fifth movement swung her left arm out and up, simultaneously pulling her left foot forward and then with one long sweeping movement her left hand almost touched the floor in the exaggerated manoeuvre.

Now the second child made her appearance with her mother following closely, then the third and so on until all the ten missing children who had been abducted by the Wolf People filed in, all with their mothers following. Approaching reverently with four movements to one side and the sweeping to the other the column advanced slowly into the open arena to the resounding voice and the roll of the ritual rattle. The slow moving column encircled the area, heaving, undulating with flowing and subsiding motions. The faces of the women lifted high in gratitude and then bowed towards the earthen floor in humility.

When the last of the children and their mothers had entered eight men appeared, each bedecked with spruce branches which warded off all evil and protected its wearers from evil spells that otherwise might have been inflicted on them. The entire column made a complete circuit around the open arena and finally stopped at the far end, next to the king's quarters. The incantation stopped and the roll of the rattle with it.

Another rattle was heard to roll from the women's section. A female voice was strong and came out with forthright boldness. It was another orison rendered up to He Who Protects All Men. The invocation was short; the woman did not repeat it. Great sparks gave forth from the cedar logs and the fire.

The troupe of ten children with their mothers and the ten braves who still stood on guard at both ends of the column presented an unusual sight made hauntingly fearsome by the silent, exaggerated movements of the dramatic entrance and the fact that the braves carried no weapons whatsoever, but relied only on the protective influence the spruce green afforded. Yet it was beautiful, it was grand, it brought a message that there was a Protector, especially so for small children.

The evergreens taken from the woods smelled so sweet, their sharp odor wafting on the warm air from the burning fires penetrated to the far corners of the great lodge. The big man with the beautifully carved rattle, his manly carriage, the tone of his strong voice, the pride that his countenance portrayed and the ten stalwart braves all produced solemnity and a grand feeling in the hearts of the onlookers, including the smaller children. Silently the company stood in front of the great throng. The children standing at an easy attention directly in front of their mothers; the braves standing alert on either side of the now half-circle.

Oomb, oomb, oomb, oomb. The thunder drums began pulsating once more. Singers, men and women alike, stood and then moved to the sides when the song leader commenced extolling in a loud voice the first bars of the song that was going to be sung, and when the actual melody burst forth the small children began keeping time and were soon giving thanks with their hands out, palms up, first one side then the other . . . one, two, three, four. . . .

With its one continuous beat the song was sung four times with brief rest periods for the young dancers. One, two, three, four movements to the right then four like movements to the left, the dance swung back and forth with up and down slow motions of gratitude used by all Indians of the coast of British Columbia to give or show thanks unto their Provider of All Wants.

The song was especially loud and strong because such a great number of the audience stood up to participate; so much so that a number of the guests from other tribes stood up to help so that the very foundations of the lodge should be "lifted" with the enthusiasm of the spirit. All the small children were drawn in, coaxed, wheedled and soothed, not with sweet sounding words but with sweet sounding songs, to become an actual part of the whole affair and readily absorbed themselves into the simple yet very important dance which they may have quite unconsciously felt was their own. They felt happy because they were an important part of the entire proceedings; their little faces shone with joy and their big black eyes sparkled with excitement.

From the day the little girls discovered they could stand up, their mothers began teaching them this dance that was especially meant for all females to perform one time or another. Little girls could do this dance before they could walk. Now it was not new to the girls. They danced beautifully. But the boys were used to more vigorous movements like the war or the victory dances. In this one they were shy and merely swayed side to side keeping time with the beat of the thunderdrums.

GIVING THANKS

It is they, it is they.   We have seen their faces.
This we know, there is no further need to seek
They have come back from the House of Qwha-yha-tseek.*
Us-ma, our loved and revered ones are with us again
For the mothers and the fathers whose hearts were sore
We lift our voices and our hearts grow strong once more.

To the ten stalwart braves whom you now see before us
We voice our thanks from the depths of our hearts.
They have not rested since the Wolf People invaded us,
They have not seen their couch of evergreens.
They went forth into the forests and beyond
In search of your Us-ma and also mine.

Hardships were met and overcome with the courage,
The cunning and wisdom that is theirs alone.
There has been no sleep for these men of courage,
There has been no comfort in the nights that were long,
There has been no food to break the fast,
There has been no water to slake the thirst.

*Wolf people.

59

Four days have come and are gone again
Since these men sallied forth in search of your own.
The night that makes four is now at hand.
This is the night that you will keep in mind.
From the land far beyond the wood and our ken
These stalwart braves snatched your Us-ma from the den.

The greens from the bough of the hemlock
Have washed the smell of the den from our Us-ma,
The sharp greens from the bough of the spruce
Have provided the means to ward off the evil
From the ghosts that may linger around its very bole
To fortify them through their journey to the wild.

Safely they are back inside the lodge that is strong.
This is the time to do good and no wrong.
The sprig of the hemlock and the spruce
Take the place which is good, full of grace.
Us-ma is back in the lodge with us all.
Us-ma has offered the Dance of Gratitude this night.

Arise now, you people of this clan,
This is a time to make merry.
Our children were taken to the House of Qwha-yha-tseek,
They have come back, we must paint their cheeks.
Lift the thunder-drum now, take it with pride,
Lift, with your voice, the foundations of this lodge.

Qwha-yha-tseek, the Wolf, failed to see our ruse
So your Us-ma was snatched from harm and abuse.
Stand now and clap your hands with joy,
Stand now with your girl and your boy,
Lift up your voice beyond this wall of cedar planks,
Lift up His song of praise and give Him thanks.

It was the speaker of the House who spoke these words.
More men and more women rose to stand with the children
and their mothers, more thunder-drums throbbed forth with
the song. There was joy and gladness in the lodge with the
earthen floor and vaulted roof.

The song leader stood tall with his eagle feathers cleaving
the air, the drummers stood two deep on either side of him.

At a given cue the drums throbbed forth their mellow beat. . . . oomb-OOMB . . . oomb-OOMB. This beat was quite different from the previous numbers in that it came in two beats, a pause, then two more, the first beat being weaker than the second which was emphatically pronounced.

oomb-OOMB . . . oomb-OOMB.

It was the king's song of thank-offering to his God, the Provider of All Wants. Its dance had the same movements as the one used during the dancers dramatic entrance a little time before, but instead of swinging their arms up and down all the women and girls kept their hands in front of them, four swings to the right then the exaggerated swing to the left, first facing forwards then backwards — one-two . . . one-two. The men did a slow march carrying in their arms, so as to show them to the best possible advantage, the king's head-dresses, masks and other paraphernalia that would be used and displayed during their own dances, plays and games at a later time. These were made manifest to the throng to attest to his complete desire to acknowledge in public the gratitude he felt for the wealth granted him and for the joy that was in his heart.

The dancers moved slowly. Around the great hall they moved and as the line progressed the women who were already dancing would dart out to snatch any young girl who was too shy to join in on her own, with good humor to pull her into the line. In a short time the line became two deep as it moved forward around the great open space and many of the younger children felt for the first time the thrill of being a part of the whole.

Remaining at the front were the ten children, their mothers and the ten braves moving and swaying with the throb of the drums but not going around with the throng. They were the object of this display of gratitude and thank offering.

The swaying promenade encircled the great lodge, completely surrounding the honored troupe who wore the greens of the spruce and the hemlock. When this was done the song ended slowly until the last note was lost into the earthen floor, the hissing fire in the middle of the lodge predominating all sounds once more.

THANKSGIVING

Choo Why Tligh, choo why tligh.   Hear ye once more.
Thanks, many thanks to all you people of this clan
    and others
For the brave way you have responded and stood with
    the mothers.
Thanks to the brave of this tribe who risked their lives
To journey forth into the land of the Wolves
While you and I stayed home by the fire with our songs.

Thanks, many thanks for the way you carried out the plan
That was the ruse born within the council of your clan.
The elders found it hard to agree with this strategy,
It was not easy for you to follow us with all honesty.
With a song you raised your voice above the drum
While you prayed in your hearts they would come.

The people of the Wolf clan failed to see the ruse,
They came to see the great fires in our house,
To gloat, sit in the deep of the wood in the dark,
They marvelled and wondered at the living aurora of
    the spark
As it burst forth into the night through the hole at the top
To rend asunder the dark and so on to the stars
    without stop.

Qwha-yha-tseek with his clan was lured from his den
When you kindled your fire at the front with cedar wood
Qwha-yha-tseek relaxed for awhile the vigil for his prize
When the throb of the drum stole through the wood
    to his den.
Qwha-yha-tseek hears all tidings, sees all things, it is said
He saw you dance outside and also saw you come inside.

Qwha-yha-tseek, the wolf, had our loved ones secure.
There was naught that we could do, he thought,
So bold and reckless, sate with brashness

He showed himself across the river in the rushes.
Ten stalwart braves of this clan, do you hear,
Into the night stole forth for your Us-ma dear.

Thanks, many thanks for the way you came through
When fears for your loved ones grew by the hour.
Thanks, many thanks for the trust that you showed
When you this ruse did carry through.
The time has come to be merry and gay.
The time has come to frolic and play.

VI

As the mist returned to the river and stole into the patch of green and into the wood the call of the wolf sounded again. This time there was a different note creeping in; the bold and challenging call was not there, instead, there was a melancholy implication brewed and mixed somewhere in the long-drawn-out howl. Nevertheless the call, borne on the eerie mist of the river, came the usual four times before the last weakening howl from a great distance away was swallowed up in the night.

The Moon of Little Sister was not there now and the stars shone brightly through the cold crisp air of night. The children with their mothers went home with the throng to rest and to sleep, secure again with their own.

This was the fifth day of the great Potlatch. The people were called to the lodge at the break of dawn when the first hint of gray yawned through from the east. Four huge fires blazed warmly in their hearths; there was no smoke to permeate the air; there were no sparks to scare the children away. A friendly atmosphere prevailed throughout the great lodge with a steady hum of subdued voices above the hiss of the fire.

The old man with the black cane appeared once again. He walked to the centre of the open area, looking around the four sides where the people sat waiting for the new day to begin. His face shone with contentment; there was a noticeable spring in his otherwise sluggish gait; there was merriment in his every movement. All sounds from the throng stopped, escaping through the smoke-hole, when the black cane was raised, but still he uttered no sound.

"Play, gambol, romp, buffoon, frolic, be merry. Anything you wish to do, you have concession to do during the coming days that number four. This we heard from the speaker of this House during the eventide of yesterday when the evening star was settling down to coax the stars to shed their light on the narrow lanes of white sea-shells that lead to the lodge where the thunder-drums throb throughout the day. Qwha-yha-tseek, from the clan of the Wolf at that time, too, took their leave to their far-off land beyond the spruce and pine. Now the sun is coming up from the east, the day has come, let us play."

The old man's voice was surprisingly loud and clear; he spoke with a lilt as he tapped the earthen floor with his black cane.

There was fun, there was laughter, there was tomfoolery throughout the day. Nobles and aristocrats mixed freely with the throng. Solos, duets and trios were heard, there was a play and there was time set aside for men to tell the biggest lies they could invent on the spot. There was no lack of contestants or participants in this doubtful amusement. Comics, troupes, large and small, paraded past the throng, amusing and entertaining it in their own improvised way. The speaker of the clan teamed up with the mentor and sang a rambling collection of the ballads and love songs of their youth.

The artisan, builder of beautiful crafts, came in backwards thumping on his drum, inducing, coaxing, wheedling his wife, who was dressed like a robin, to come in with him. When she did appear, very shyly at first, she stood at the door with her enormous breast as red as it was buxom uncertain which way to go, a huge black eye shining, her black head cocked to the floor, listening intently for the worm to betray itself above the earth. Presently she took a sudden sail that consisted of a few rapid choppy steps and stopped to cock her black head to the other side, always listening intently for that worm. It was remarkable how well the choppy measured movements of the bird fitted the lyrics of the Robin Song.

Seemingly an endless variety of plays, dances and general nonsense paraded in and around the great lodge. Almost all the animals and birds that were in the kingdom were imitated or represented in one form or another.

A staid and venerable man who was the best whale hunter ambled in as if from nowhere. His costume was all black from the head, which showed no eyes, to oversized feet. He waddled aimlessly to the huge fire in the middle of the arena, hopped on a black rock that was conveniently near, lifted his small head with its long tapering black beak and looked hither and yon to make sure that no one was peeping, shook his scraggy tail, spread out two black wings and began sunning himself. He was the shag.

Two corpulent people marched resolutely to the centre of the arena and began having uncontrollable convulsions of laughter, the tears streaming down their ruddy faces. At first it appeared and sounded too ridiculous to watch but presently a buxom woman who was a spectator began laughing also and it was not long before the entire throng was in stitches of laughter.

A long sleek figure appeared from the shadows, his costume was a rich brown and he had extremely short limbs. He was on all fours and loped in long graceful leaping movements on an erratic course, stopping abruptly now and again to rise most gracefully on his short hind legs and search the horizon of his vision, conspicuously displaying a gleaming white vest, only to settle again, arching his handsome long body as he resumed the loping motion. Presently he espied a woman who sat near the front of the audience, strutted brazenly to her side, rose arrogantly and stretched himself to an astonishing height and began to make naughty, if not atrocious, advances to her, whispering in her ear, stroking her hair and trying adroitly to reach her hand, all the while displaying his beauti-ful white vest. When his advances were not encouraged he moved on to the next woman and so on until he lost himself again in the shadows. He was the mink.

In the Indian legends the mink was the fickle, handsome Lothario of the animal kingdom.

A troupe of comely young women flitted in, their cheeks painted a bright sparkling blue. Each wore a headdress with a long blue bill, large blue eyes and a long spike that stuck out saucily from the crown towards the back. The whole headdress was painted with the same sparkling blue. The troupe flitted in swiftly and with purpose. They started their imagined flight high on their toes and finished low on their knees most gracefully. The troupe represented a company of blue-jays.

This was followed immediately by yet another company of young women. Their cheeks were painted white and they wore beautiful white head coverings made entirely from white feathers. They sailed in noisily, wheeling and screaming with the high pitched call of the seagulls they were depicting. They were the company of the seagull clan. Their headdresses were said to be made from the whole coat of that bird, peeled off and dried in the sun.

A company of young men who had gathered in a tight knot near the far end of the arena dispersed to reveal a pile of rocks and on top of the pile a dumpy, fat little figure, squatting on his heels. His short nose with long spiky whiskers was pointed high and stayed poised, perfectly still. He was the marmot.

An enormous big and well-built man rushed in from out-side and between panting and gasping for breath he told the throng that on his way from his house he had espied a big wolf asitting on his haunches in the wood, watching with live and glinting eyes every move the merrymakers made.

"We must be careful and do no evil for he may be the

watchman sent by the clan of the Wolf People. We must be extremely careful."

The man appeared to be completely serious as he punctuated the words and finished his short announcement by saying that if for any reason the clan of Wolf People became displeased by any show or hint of licentious, erotic or dishonorable behavior, it was said they would come back and raid the entire village with vengeance. The big man left reluctantly and appeared to be nervous and uncertain where to go. This information struck fear and perhaps anguish into the hearts of the young who were in the lodge.

A kindly man ambled into the arc of light from the bright fire nearest to the end where the children were sitting. He was not tall but looked very big. He was a jovial looking man, perhaps because of his ruddy complexion and enormous smile that revealed small, even teeth and a mischievious twinkle in his soft brown eyes. Without any introduction, or any explanation of his intention, he began in a quiet soothing voice.

"Long ago, I do not remember when, the human people had no fire. But the Wolf People had fire! The Wolf People were dreaded by all and no others could have the fire. The Wolf People guarded their fire well and no human was able to capture even a tiny spark, no matter how hard they tried. The humans were in despair. The winters were cold. Then one day Ah-tush-mit, the tiny deer, said to the great chief, 'I'll get you the fire'."

By this time all those who could possibly get near to the old man were crowding around him, listening intently as they stared into the huge fire burning in front of them.

The man took his time. He told of the secret plan of the tiny Ah-tush-mit, the Son of Deer, and how he danced for the dreaded wolves in their own great lodge where they kept and guarded their precious fire so well, and he executed the actual dance the little deer had performed, hopping straight up and down as he sidled towards the site of an imagined fire opposite to the real one that burned merrily to their right, and singing all the while Ah-tush-mit's little ditty in a small, small voice. "Khi-yahhh tlin tlin tlin tlin. . . ."

The old man hopped up and down keeping time with his hands as he clapped out the beat of the funny little tune. He told how the tiny Son of Deer hopped and sailed over the roaring fire of the Wolf People and how his little knees caught a spark of the fire and how he sped home to the human people with the spark.*

All the children sat completely captivated, forgetting the dread that had crept into their little hearts only a few moments before. The old man was the village story-teller.

Many, many more plays and dances were shown and performed. It seemed endless. The four days sped by and the time arrived much too soon when they must stop the nonsense and return to normal behavior.

*This tale is told in detail in *Son of Raven, Son of Deer*, George Clutesi, Gray's Publishing Ltd., Sidney, B.C.

VII

THE TLOO-QWAH-NAH

Choo-why, to honored guests, one and all,
The Moon of Little Sister waxes stronger still;
The winds from the north will bring the chill;
The autumn night frost has come to stay a spell.
Our hearts became whole, we were free, we were gay
For your young, in mine house, did frolic and play.

On the morrow, when the sun to the east
Pulls over yon hills, all frolic and the jest
Will fade away, only fond reflections to recall.
In its place will come our songs of ritual,
The dance, the play of great import to us all.
This inheritance, we must not let fall.

For remainder of the time, this House would now say,
All things that are small, from your mind put away.
No room will there be, for small things in this plan;
Show now that which is good, for your own clan.
All evil put away, restrain and watch your plays
When, in this House you show your rituals.

In your mind always keep our fortune, that was good
When our loved ones returned from the wood
In four short days, not ten or never at all.
In your mind always keep the obligations that we owe
To honored guests in this House that is your own,
To the clan that made you proud to belong.

The rising sun on the morrow will mark the time.
Ten plus two, by the count of ancient lore,
When this House commenced to do the play.
Deep rooted laws of our forebears, we will obey.
When on the morrow, the portals you pass under
Stay beside the fire and make no blunder.

Qwha-yha-tseek, the wolf was on the prowl, our Us-ma stole
When we became bold and thus became frail.
We must always the vigil keep;   we must always
          remain calm.
Strengthen the spirit and comfort the limb
For on the morrow and 'till the last day come
You will sup in this lodge, I make my home.

THE SPEAKER OF THE TRIBE was firm and resolute in his instructions to his clan. He was serious, the humor of yesterday
was not there. He was speaking for the author of this great
play, the Tloo-qwah-nah.

"You have heard the speaker of our clan; you know now
what we must do. Starting on the morrow when you have
been summoned to this lodge by the village crier, who you
know, stay inside and do not go out of doors for any reason
unless you are sent on an errand. Break well your fast in the
morning at the lodge in which you stay for you will be, by
tradition, required to stay beside the fires until the rituals
of the day are put away. Starting on the morrow, all noon-
hour meals and those for eventide will be served in this lodge
for you to enjoy.

"This day marks ten plus one since this House, through its
portals called you in. We played with a will, there were no
days lost. The days that numbered four came swiftly and
were gone again. We enjoyed ballads, skits, the stories that
were told, we know now the biggest fibber in this clan.

"We are grateful for the willingness with which you offered
yourselves in the dances, plays and nonsense too. On the
morrow, we are told, all these things that are small will be left
behind for the days that are gone.

71

"Strengthen now the spirit, we are told, for on the morrow we will paint our faces and apply the color for the play.

"The fires wane low which indicates that it is time for us to go home and rest awhile for the day. Get a good night's sleep. Starting on the morrow there will be little sleep; starting on the morrow there is much work to be done. We do assure our honored guests that your respective hosts will take care of your comfort. Go now and rest awhile."

The old man with the black cane was formal in this his address to the throng. Seldom he became this serious for he was widely known throughout the coast for his good humor.

There was, indeed, much work to be done both inside the great lodge and outside as well. The cedar mat partitions that were taken down, prior to the attack of the wolves on that fateful night when ten small children were abducted and taken captive, were put back into place; the four fires were put out, all excessive ashes removed, and relit again one at a time; the wood was replenished and stacked in the two corners nearest to the great doors.

A team of four young men were on the roof replacing boards around the smoke-holes that had been burned during the great spurts of fire that were made in an effort to deter and perhaps drive back the marauding wolves from the lodge. The women were busy sweeping and cleaning the great open area of the expansive earthen floors.

Traditionally, no green branch of any conifer or evergreen was ever put into a fire so all broken bits of spruce and hemlock that littered the floors were gathered up and taken out of doors so that in time they could return to the earth from whence they came.

The day that marked ten plus two since the inception of this Tloo-qwah-nah, dawned clear, cold and crisp. The night frost embraced the tree limbs that were now naked of all foliage, blanketing them from the wind that would come from the north.

The Moon of Little Sister was due to enter phase two. She had remained in the western sky late into the night before, reluctant to pull herself down and out of sight although she had every morn witnessed the opening of each day.

Promptly at the break of dawn the people, the hosts and the guests, filed into the great lodge. All the womenfolk carried robes for their guests because this was the day when one must not leave the fireside until all things were put away for the day.

The four fires blazed invitingly and showed no smoke with the right amount of logs cribbed onto them. There was no need of whale oil for these fires. The great lodge filled rapidly, the people taking their seats in accordance with the usher's directions. This posed no unnecessary delay as they were all returned to their own places allotted to them on the first day. The members of the council who occupied or owned their special seats were already in their places when the people started coming in, for it was the duty of these men to set the example and any tardiness was frowned upon as a sign of indecorum. All offenders were reprimanded by the village crier.

A distinguished-looking and handsome woman moved slowly forward from the inner chambers and stopped opposite that of the author or giver of the Tloo-qwah-nah who had also moved forward from his seat amongst the councillors.

The two met momentarily but the man immediately moved to the woman's right and turned deliberately until he was facing the throng also. The ceremonial rattle that the woman carried in her left hand began its roll imperceptibly at first, but soon its sound increased with the rich clear voice that rendered the incantation, the prayer-song, the orison to the Provider of All Wants.

No other sound could be heard in the packed lodge. All eyes were fixed respectfully on the woman who led the tall handsome man as they turned slowly to face the four directions of the wind beyond the four cedar walls of the great lodge. This was in accordance with their ancient laws to acknowledge the four powers* and also the four seasons that make and complete one cycle of their thirteen moons.

"Gaze now upon his countenance. This is the man whose voice you have heard and will hear throughout the duration of this Tloo-qwah-nah. This is the man whose lodge the Qwha-yha-tseek, from the clan of the wolves, honored by their visit the other night when they carried our children away. This is the man who mastered the plot that foiled the wolves and rescued the children before harm could befall any one of them. This is the man who prepared and arranged for the days that numbered four when you flung your cares to the four winds of this our land and recalled the days when you were young with a song in your heart.

"It is so. His voice has been heard, yea his voice will come in many more modes and manners when he makes utterance in this House.

"Gaze now into his face. When he stands before you look not away.

"This is the day when we must comply with the laws laid down by the ancestors that made you, this man, and his House. If for some reason you do not subscribe to the tenets of the Tloo-qwah-nah you now have his blessings to leave this his lodge and come no more until you are summoned, if ever.

"Young men, in twos, are now ready with their horn and jar of black paint to serve you and color your cheek. I would remind you that this is the first law we must observe from now on until the last day comes. We must distinguish our own from those who do not belong to the society of the Tloo-qwah-nahs.

"Mothers, guardians and elders we would now advise you to prepare your young to stand and be counted with the color upon their cheek. Rest well and easy, comfort your

*Indian religion adds a grandchild to the trinity.

limbs; this day marks the time when the ceremonies will commence."

The woman was an elder sister of the man she had presented to the throng. Both returned to their seats to await the paint to color their cheeks.

The four fires blazed invitingly. There was no smoke.

Four teams of young men went around the great lodge applying the black to both cheeks of young and old. One held the pot of black paint while the other applied the color. There was no special ceremony involved in the simple application of color. Nevertheless it was, as explained, that all who wished to stay with the throng to participate or sit and watch must show this badge of the society.

All went well. All the people, especially the young, were eager to show the color upon their cheek, proud to belong to the Tloo-qwah-nahs. The application was simple. Two fingers into the pot of paint, a quick dab on both cheeks and it was over, and so on to the next. The four teams were rapidly finishing their chores — a pleasant duty they enjoyed doing, perhaps because the smaller children were so eager and loved to have their faces blackened.

The ten children who had been abducted by the Qwha-yha-tseek from the clan of wolves were allowed to stay and have their faces painted black too. This was a great experience for them because now, for the first time in their lives, they really "belonged" to the throng and perhaps because everybody else was happy they too were very happy and nestled closer to their mothers. While the painting of faces was being carried out the womenfolk began to sing and do the Dance of Gladness at the end where the children were sitting. All went well.

The old man with the black cane stepped forward and moved towards the young men who were now applying color to each other's cheeks. All were in high spirits. This day marked the commencement of the Tloo-qwah-nah. All went well. The young men, numbering eight, were now standing near the great doors, blocking it because of their number.

The man with the cane walked directly to them and consulted with them briefly and began shaking his head as he held up one finger; his index finger pointed straight up, indicating one.

All of a sudden he appeared to be very agitated. He turned to the throng holding his slender cane up in front of him cross-ways and edged towards the great doorway, indicating that no one in the lodge could leave, go out, or pass the immediate ground he now stood on.

The black cane was a symbol of the old man's office as village master of ceremonies and interpreter to the speaker of the clan. This office carried much honor and much authority. No one belonging to the House, clan or tribe dare challenge or show disrespect to this old man — not when he carried his black cane.

No one moved. No one spoke. There was silence in the throng.

"Three hundred and ninety nine heads entered this lodge this morning at the break of dawn. Three hundred and ninety eight heads were marked with the paint that is the badge of the Tloo-qwah-nah Society. There is one that did not come forward. Rise now and be marked. This is a law that we must obey. Rise!"

No one rose. Instead a low hum from the throng issued forth and was felt rather than heard. No one made a move.

The old man with the black cane nodded his head to the eight young men who were now standing resolutely on either side of him. The eight stalwarts immediately moved forward, deploying four men to the lateral sides of the lodge who moved forward cautiously. Their eyes were searching for the missing one. They counted heads as they moved along, missing no one. No one spoke. There was silence.

The searching team was midway along the sides of the lodge when a lone figure was seen to detach himself away from the guests. He moved with ease as he sidled into the open arena facing the eight stalwart young men who had now espied him. Immediately they deployed and fanned out in an effort to encircle him so that he might be marked with black paint.

The man was small, slight in build, with a ruddy complexion and extremely black hair that was knotted at the top of his small head. This signified that he was ready for the last stand in a battle, or in his efforts to escape the cordon of stalwarts bearing down on him at this moment. He moved easily but he moved with extreme agility and speed as he cautiously backed away, looking, searching for an opening through which he might slip. He crouched low near the earthen floor, now touching it with his fingers, perhaps hoping desperately that it would enclose him into its silent darkness. The eight young braves closed in relentlessly. Slowly but surely they advanced to reduce the gap, the distance that separated them from this insurgent, this rebel who dared to defy ancient laws. The man was soon backed against the far wall that separated the king's quarters. He was cornered.

All knew that he dare not enter the great personage's chambers. He must surrender and give himself up for the marking. He stood still crouching lower and lower until he was on his haunches, the tips of his fingers touching the earthern floor as if to receive his deliverance from it. No one spoke. There was silence in the throng.

The men, now confident of a quick success, moving on silent feet were coming in with their pot of black paint, remaining upright. No need to crouch. This was going to be easy. There were enough of them to catch a slight, small man. Suddenly he darted to the left, covering the wide width of the area in rapid, short steps, his small feet barely lifting off the earthen floor. He moved so swiftly that the oncoming cordon of men stood momentarily startled by his incredible speed.

With little trouble the small man had evaded the initial

efforts at capture. He was now at the far side of the lodge. His arms, which were abnormally long for his height, were now held at an angle, touching the packed earthen floor, feeling it, caressing it with the tip of his thin fingers, moving, hugging the earth, as it were, with his outstretched arms.

The men moved swiftly now that they had seen the agility of their intended victim and closed in resolutely to clamp him down bodily on the floor to apply the black paint. He crouched now with his back to the side of the great lodge, unable to retreat any farther. The cordon tightened, attempting to encircle him. The man stood his ground, eyeing his assailants without turning his head. No one spoke. There was silence in the throng.

For the first time the throng really saw the man that was the object of this chase. He appeared to be small, smaller because he hugged the floor. He wore no garments save for a tight loin-cloth. There he crouched, perfectly motionless, the light from the fire nearest him playing upon his cheekbones that were high and extremely prominent. His mouth he held in a tight straight line. His eyes were mere slits but nevertheless full of fire reflected from the burning fires on either side of him. There was determination on his face. He was not going to be caught. He was not going to be marked.

He stood now against the raised low platform that ran around three sides of the great lodge. This portion was the marking point between public and private areas. No one dared, without invitation, to infringe this privilege. It was a law that all knew; to keep out of that area unless placed there by the usher during a feast or at a Potlatch. Accordingly the man avoided that area. He avoided going near where the children were sitting with their mothers. The young men who were bent on marking him knew he would do this so they felt that because his manoeuvres would be restricted to the open area of the earthen floor it would be relatively simple to pin him down for the marking. Swiftly now the cordon tightened.

Still the man made no move. The pursuers now closed in with their arms outstretched to cover more area as they cornered the elusive, rebellious man. No one spoke. There was silence everywhere.

Without warning, the man darted to his right and like a streak he sped to his left. The cordon moved with his first manoeuvre but before they could recover and shift back the man was gone. He was not there. He had sprung forward without breaking his easy flowing movements and slipped under a hand that held one of the pots of black paint. Now he was down at the far end of the lodge racing towards the old man with the black cane held crossways in front of him guarding the only exit from the lodge but at a safe distance he turned abruptly away. He faced his pursuers, now leaning forward at an astonishing angle that necessitated continual motion on his part. He was on his toes. He slipped to one side, now to the other — moving, moving, moving.

The old man made no effort whatsoever to interfere or help the young men in catching the rebel other than to remain in front of the doorway with his black cane.

Until now the pursuers had refrained from running or show-ing any indication of extra effort other than to bear down on the man in their numbers and corner him, but now it was evi-dent that they were losing their patience with this foolishness. Both men who carried the pots of paint now placed their small but unwieldy receptacles onto the low platform and joined their comrades who were reforming their line for a ruthless bodily charge upon the shifty target so as to clamp him to the floor and smear black paint on his whole face. The cordon came in swiftly to surround the now dancing object of their pursuit. Each man was crouching low, advancing in a dog-trot with menacing fingers outstretched, swinging freely as they closed in on the slight dancing figure on his tiptoes.

The dancing, moving figure was continuously sidling until he was in the middle of the great arena. There was no fear showing on his resolute countenance. He was determined to make his escape. Or would he dare to make a stand? Instantly the cordon tightened for the final rush, coming in low to the floor. Like a flash the small figure feigned a drop to the floor but before anyone realized what had happened he sprang, like a mountain lion, up and onto the back of one of the crouching figures that was near to the middle of the open area. The man instinctively threw himself upright, violently catapulting the leaping figure up and up until his outstretched arms slammed violently against a crossbeam of the lodge and he swung under, over and onto the beam in one graceful movement.

The figure scurried onto a main lateral beam. He was on all fours because of the extreme lowness of the roof above his head.

"Smoke-hole! Close the smoke-hole! He's heading for the smoke-hole!" The leader of the team yelled the words between gasps.

Instead of going for the narrow slits at the ridge of the great lodge the figure scurried on the main beam until he was near the old man with the black cane and dropped down, landing on his toes and springing down to cushion the violent descent of his body. Before his pursuers could collect themselves the slight figure was standing calmly in front of the old man with the black cane who promptly applied, most respectfully, the black mark to his cheeks.

A woman stepped out briskly from the near side and her rattle rolled with resolution but she faltered, because of her pent up emotions, before her voice came forth with her own incantation. No one intruded the sacred orison and the tension that had built up to breaking point was shattered. An audible sigh of relief went up. The fires were rekindled and burned invitingly on their hearths.

As the old man with the black cane had put the black paint on the cheeks of the defiant one he whispered under his breath.

"Well done Kah-oots, my grandchild. You are a brave."

For the young man was indeed his grandson.

"You could easily have made your escape through the smoke-hole but you chose to honor your old Nah-neek-so, grandparent, instead by receiving the color from his own hand. I am proud of you."

The young man made no reply. There was no need to. His surrender to the grand old master of ceremonies was ample proof of his respect for the aged and indeed for ancient laws. He carried the color with pride as he was led back to his own seat by his grandfather.

The old man was his jolly self again as he made his way back to the far end of the lodge where the dignitaries sat, and upon reaching the area he turned to face the throng.

"The beginning of this important affair was marred by the insolence of one of our own members who rebelled against carrying the mark. That was not good. You saw his speed and extreme agility. We marvelled at his adroitness, his dexterity and his skill to evade capture. He had indeed escaped for he could have slipped out of the smoke-hole at the top but he did not. He chose to surrender and comply with the law. Let it be said that we are fortunate to have a man of his abilities in our midst. All went well then, let us say."

The great fires were stoked and blazed invitingly.

Ah-mah, The Loon

VIII

THIS MARKED THE FIRST FORMAL FEAST in the lodge since the commencement of the great gathering of the ten clans. It was given by the elder sister of the author of the Tloo-qwah-nah, the one who opened it and presented him to the throng. There was no special or significant announcement that the elder sister was the hostess of the affair save by word of mouth.

Qwah-niss, the camas bulbs that had been dried and buried in sand since early spring had been carefully warmed in hot water. This food was now being served from huge wooden feast dishes that were carried by two young men while a third served it out into large gleaming white clam-shells. When the steaming bulbs of the camas reached the clans from the coastal area there were loud exclamations of approval because this was indeed a treat to them. Especially so at this time of year.

"Choooo chu chu chu chu choh," was heard from many of the guests as the Qwah-niss was dipped liberally into seal oil that was placed beside each serving. This was indeed a treat. Tleets-upe and Ah-ee-tso were also served and their crunchy meat made a welcome contrast to the mushiness of the Qwah-niss.

The old man did not sit down to eat. He moved around the great throng overseeing the serving of the delicacies, joking good-naturedly and keeping the guests happy and in good spirits.

Long beforehand it had been common knowledge that the

elder sister would act as host for the initial feast of the Tloo-qwah-nah. When the day arrived all the guests had remembered to bring a large wooden basin for the Mah-moot, the important left-over, that was intentionally served so it might be taken home for later meals or given to those who did not attend the feast.

The young men who were especially schooled to do this service were kept busy taking the Mah-moot to the homes in wooden basins. During all feasts, extreme care was taken to ensure that no individual was left out or forgotten. A feast was for all; from the nobles to the meanest slave, in spite of the law that no slaves should attend or be present when the Tloo-qwah-nah proper commenced. All owners or masters of slaves were honor bound to make provisions for their charges on these occasions. Many basins of Qwah-niss and oils were taken home for the Mah-moot.

Feasts were the time for making speeches. Feasts were the best time to orate, teach, give an opinion, or merely voice thanks to your hosts. It was said, it was believed, that one absorbed and received more knowledge when eating and swallowing food. One was more receptive to opinions, convictions, tenets, tribal history and the telling of ancient tales when one was chewing and swallowing. This was the belief of all coastal clans.

The speakers of the various clans rose, one by one, and expressed their deep gratitude for all the good things that had been bestowed unto their august parties, their esteemed women-folk, their revered young and to their Mus-chim, the common man, without which no House, no clan, no tribe could be or indeed exist. Many beautiful thoughts were expressed in beautiful words.

The man with the soft speaking voice was the last man to rise. Like his predecessors he was in high spirits and he skill-fully injected humor into his opening remarks.

"Suspect, do I, that the oil of the seal which is so precious

84

was meted out in liberal measure to oil the larynx that is in want of volume — much more volume. I have partaken of your precious oils but the larynx is still feeble." He said more and he skilfully used and availed himself of the especially high spirits of the throng, always directing the jokes to himself and enjoying immensely the laughter that he produced.

The West Coast Indians were widely noted for their eloquence, for their philosophical views and opinions of their tenets and creeds and for their innate ability to deliver and express their thoughts most beneficially. Indeed it was unpardonable to hurt or embarrass another person in public by careless talk or effrontry for it was a direct reflection of the lack or rejection of all teachings. They were also noted for their deep sense of humor and the appreciation of merriment and laughter.

QWAH-NISS FEAST

Gracious hostess of this lodge, let me speak again
The days are few when one can sit and stare
To marvel at so many deeds of a House.
Your food so good no other can compare
Long have I wished the Qwah-niss[1] to taste
Which this day I enjoyed with relish.

Nine moons ago the great spawn left us
That was the time to harvest the Qwah-niss
When the hostess of this lodge dug for hers
To save for us throughout the summer moons.
Look how we now share this food so rare
Rest assured we are grateful for this regard.

Indeed it is true that our hostess is Hah-cumb[2]
The womenfolk respond to her call.   It is clear
That her clan serve her well.   We can see
Her House is never in want, that is sure.
This dish so delectable is her own to enjoy
Yet we share the Qwah-niss at this time.

[1] Camas bulb.
[2] Queen.

85

When our hearts are filled with gladness
We lift the drums to frolic and play
When we sit and eat food without shame
This Qwah-niss that belongs to your land
We know we shall hear your songs again
And witness your plays and dances too.

We marvel at the voices more and more
That come from this House and your tribe
Rest easy our attention you will keep
Be assured we are with you as of yore
This is the time to renew our friendship
Our clan is your ally, as yours to mine.

We keep in mind the reason for this call
We know the true intent of the Tloo-qwah-nah.
The Ten Tribes in this lodge from near and far
Are here to show our strong alliance
We are grateful indeed for your kindness
Thanks, many thanks, are due you and your clan.

With these words the speaker with the soft speaking voice ended his address to the hostess of the feast.

It was late in the winter's evening when the last speaker had resumed his seat with the throng. The great fires were not replenished with wood, indicating that in a short time all things would be put away for the day.

The West Coast Indian hurried not in any undertaking. At a meal, at a feast, he took much time. He hurried not. There was time, much time for everything in his life. He ate two good meals a day; a hearty breakfast and a big meal before retiring at night. It was a widespread belief that hunger prior to sleep induced fear of want. Little children were fed before bedtime so that they would not have dreams of hunger or nightmares.

There was a great variety of foods available to the Coast Indian but he was wont to partake of them one course at a time. If, for instance, as in the first feast he had Qwah-niss, he had that alone or with other root-stocks that were related and nothing more save the oils that he used extensively with staples.

With the long meal of this first feast and the orations of the many guest speakers the people had sat still throughout the long day with no opportunity to stretch their legs. The master of ceremonies, the old man with the black cane, had relented and informed the throng to gather their robes and go home to retire for the night as all things had been put away for the day.

Except for the incantations, the Welcome Song, the Opening Song, and the Song of Gratitude when the ten abducted children were returned, all the songs, plays and dances were performed in the spirit of fun, humor and light comedy. Now it had changed to an extreme ritualistic essence. serious

All songs that would be used henceforward must "belong" to the singer, dancer or performer in accordance with long established axioms. This did not create any unfavorable situations because of the extreme co-operative inclinations of all Coastal Indians. Indeed the owners of songs freely offered their numbers to their relatives no matter how remote to be used whenever possible.

Members of a House had the privilege of using any song that belonged to that particular House. The only requirement was that he inform the presiding council of his intention during the planning stage which most often lasted one full cycle of the seasons — one year. Likewise the head of that House had the right to refuse or otherwise dissuade the use of any song, dance or play, which did occur on remote occasions. If, for instance, death had occurred in that particular House at a time which was considered too close to the festivities then all festive songs that the deceased would have used had he been alive were put away for a period of a full cycle of the thirteen moons. Because of this understanding and during such mourning periods few privileges were applied for or sought.

Each and every participant of the Tloo-qwah-nah would

start his own ceremony by rendering his own incantation, songs and plays in accordance with their importance. The more important ones were always reserved for the end of the event.

During the initial period of the Tloo-qwah-nah proper many songs were sung, many dances and plays performed. The days sped by as the feasts increased in number. One family after another rose to announce their intention to join, to participate, because their hearts had been reached — moved by the songs and the rituals. There was never a slow or a dull moment during the entire Tloo-qwah-nah. The plays that were shown were varied, educational and full of interest, particularly to the younger men and women for whose benefit they were performed.

One of them occurred with no announcement whatever except, perhaps, that the four great fires were allowed to wane low on their hearths.

Haaaah ha ha ha ha ha. Haaaah ha ha ha ha ha.

A peal of feminine laughter issued forth from the shadows outside the great doors of the lodge as a comely young woman darted in, then darted hither and yon seeking the shadows, to be followed immediately by a second, a third and yet another until there were seven in all. Darting behind screens and behind round posts that had been placed the night before, ostensibly to support the huge beams, they let out peals of sensual laughter as they gained the shadows. The young women never showed themselves other than by provocative darts from one shadow to another. No laugh was heard individually, it issued forth from seven directions almost simultaneously. Each player darted behind the posts towards the place of the fires to keep out of sight of the onlookers, and behind other screens that were placed conveniently between the posts. The four fires were waning low on their hearths, the narrow smoke-holes were closed to narrow slits, blue smoke permeated the already darkened atmosphere inside the great lodge.

The performers were dressed in long flowing robes made from the inner bark of the yellow cedar; some in its natural white, some dyed red or a disturbing orange. The girls' deep-set eyes were shadowed black to and beyond their cheekbones. There was a dash of red ochre upon each cheek and their brows were arched and pencilled black to allure the young and unwary. They made no move or approach to the men, or to anyone, as they darted from one shadow to the other behind posts and screens while they sent forth disarming laughter from their concealment. The darting women made the entire round of the planted posts, never showing themselves between each seductive move, but the peals of provocative laughter never ceased. They laughed themselves out of the arena as they had come in. Haaaah ha ha ha ha ha.

"We have seen, you and I, the laughing sirens of the trees. We have been fortunate because, it is said, they are rarely seen, if ever, that they never venture beyond the forest of pine and cedar but stay in the shadows of the thicket of the wood. It is said that these women you have seen cannot think for themselves, that their minds are not their own. It is said that the women you have seen before your eyes go through life with no intent but to frolic, to make merry and to laugh. It is said that the young who fall and are seduced into their camp return not unto their own but stay with the creatures who think not and cannot reason to know what is good and what is evil. It is said that if in your ramblings you should hear this laughter in the wood behind a tree, tarry not, but turn and go the other way. It is said that this is difficult to do when one is young."

> The laughter is sweet, it tickles the heart.
> The women are comely to look at and fun to be near.
> It is said that one must be strong to turn and go the
>   other way.
> The laughter is sweet, we did hear it this night, you and I.
> It is also bitter, because he will die with it on his lips
> Should he succumb and turn not the other way.

The old man with the black cane interpreted the play in a sad, melancholy tone of voice with his lean, drawn face towards the earthen floor. He spoke to no one in particular. He seemed to be thinking aloud to himself.

The days were speeding by now. So much so that the songs, the plays and the feasts that now occurred each day at noon and late in the evening hours continued until the old man with the black cane announced that all things were to be put away for the night. The guests would amble home laden with their robes, reluctant to leave the great lodge and the warmth of the fires on the hearths.

Many more dances and plays were performed between each feast. As the days waned weaker with the rounding of the Moon of Little Sister the nights grew longer and the thunder-drums oombed farther into the night beside the fires in the lodge.

No one knew about this one play, except those whose performance it was. The vested rights rested solely with one House and family. This play was directed towards the young man who aspired to become a warrior.

In the late afternoon a large fire was kindled upon the hearth outside the lodge. The cedar logs were cribbed high to act as a chimney for the upward draft. The fire roared and spat out great sparks in all directions. There was no smoke.

A blood-curdling yell was heard outside. It penetrated the walls of the cedar planks of the lodge, instilling fear into the hearts of the little ones as they drew closer to their mothers who embraced them with both arms and assured the children that they would stay inside and not go out. All the children were made to stay inside the lodge because they were told that the people outside making the awful sounds were not good for the young to see. They were fighting.

The older men and women and all the young men filed out of the great doors to see what the din and commotion was about. Soon the open area in front of the lodge was filled with people peering into the darkness beyond the fires.

Blood-curdling yells came from the darkness beyond the arc of light from the fire in front of the lodge. A clash of whale bone clubs, bone upon bone sounded as sparks billowed into the night when the high cribbed cedar logs tumbled down into their own flames and burst with renewed force, spreading light into the far shadows. There was silence. No one moved. No one spoke. There was nothing to see. There was silence.

Slowly, painfully from the dark a lone figure emerged into the arc of light; the licking, moving long flames of the great fire cast the shadow of his forlorn, dejected figure upon a wall of thickets nearby hoary with the night frost. He uttered no word. He moved as if in pain. With effort he dragged himself into the arc of light from the fire which now seemed to roar with vengeance. The man was naked except for the loincloth that was girded tight. His eyes, now staring and seeing naught, were shadowed deep; upon his cheeks and smeared over his body was the black of war-paint.

Mutely he moved into the open from the blackness of the night. He labored under a great weight yet no pain showed upon his face. His left leg dragged and he moved with his head bent down next to the earth white with the rime of the night. He eased forward, his good foot picking its way until he was in the light of the licking fire, a desolate figure out of the night. He straightened. To his full height he stood.

Blood. His own blood trickled down from the corner of his sagging mouth, down his chin, and dripped sluggishly onto his bare chest. There it congealed because he was cold; his body was without heat. Tightly in both hands he clutched the shaft of a spear that had impaled him through the groin on his right. He had been hit in combat. His eyes burned hot with the fever that gripped him. He showed no pain upon his tired face. He stared out into the night to ward off the death that would surely come.

His eyes bulged, peering into the dark of his lonely night.
He was alone.   He saw no one.   The great fire blazed
    in the night.
The throng that watched him he saw not.
He saw nothing beyond the spear that impaled his groin,
    on his right.
Tightly, with both hands he clutched the shaft.

He would stay the hand that would come to pull it out.
Deep inside he knew that should this happen, he would die.
His face, now lifted high.   His eyes stared out into
    the night.
He moved into the night.   He was alone.

The throng that stood beside the outside fire made no move to go inside when the man with the spear impaled through his groin was lost into the night. No comments were heard, good or bad. There was silence in the throng. The young men tarried, staring into the dying fire upon the hearth. A drum oombed forth from inside the lodge. A song was heard to start with a slow steady beat that was sad. The people moved slowly and filed back into the lodge. A feast followed but the lilt of yesterday was gone. The play outside had chilled the spirit of everyone.

Some womenfolk rallied and sang a few of their ballads that yesterday would have brought everyone to his feet. Many men stood gallantly to support them but the young men sat silently staring into the fires on the hearths.

Children, who had stayed indoors, were the only ones whose voices could be heard above the low hiss of the fires as they asked what had gone on outside.

"Why does everyone look so sad? Why is everyone so quiet all of a sudden?" they asked their mothers in timid voices.

"Be patient, child, I am sure the old man with the black cane will step forward when the time comes and tell you and the throng the message of the play."

At this feast the Mah-moot that was carried to the homes by the young men of the clan was plenteous.

There it was, young men of our tribe.
You have seen for yourselves the warrior bold
There is glory for awhile, but not for long.
You saw the spear impale the groin
You saw the blood from his mouth issue forth
You saw him totter on to his death
You saw him fade into his night
Forevermore lost from our sight.

The old man was not as happy as his usual self. He was never the type to go to wars or pursue strife. This display of violence left him sad. It was not his life.

It was not often that the old man with the black cane became so formal in his speech when he was on the floor of the lodge. No doubt the play outside the lodge had disturbed him much more than he was willing to admit or make known to the throng — especially to their guests from the far-off tribes.

The feast finished with little time lost and as the fires began to wane on the hearths the people began to gather and fold their robes so that they might go home for another night's rest.

IX

BLOOD STAINED THE SKY TO THE EAST as the dawn opened this very morn. The wind from the north was not there. Small puffs of wind that whirled round and round from the bare earth beside the lodge picked up dry leaves left there in the fall and bore them on invisible wings high, high up in the air. The small gusts of wind that reached the lodge were warm. Even in the early morning the air was close, damp and sultry. There was a change in the weather to come.

The village crier knew this as he returned from his morning's ablutions at his pool deep within the wood. He scanned long the sky to the east before he called the villagers and their guests with his penetrating cry in the early morn.

"Walk now at once! Walk now at once! Let not your king alone sit in his lodge. Walk now at once, walk now at once!"

The villagers with their guests moved with some speed as they headed to the lodge, casting and lifting their eyes to the east as they pondered and sniffed an impending change in the weather. The gusts of wind now came down more and more frequently and hit their nostrils with warm moisture-laden air.

The guests filled the great lodge and sat awhile beside the fires guessing, wondering what this new day would bring. One day, so far, was never like the last nor any other. Fires burned forebodingly, sputtering with black smoke.

Whoo-Whyyyyyyy!   Whoo-Whyyyyyyy!

Whoo-Whyyyyyyy!   Whoo-Whyyyyyyy!

A call for help? A desperate call for help? Or was it the
wind from the north that did not come with the morn? Within
the lodge no man knew for sure what it was. The plaintive cry
did not come again. It was the wind from the north?

The old man with the black cane detached himself from
the area of the councillors. His lean face looked haggard. He
was tired. He carried his cane crosswise in front of him. He
spoke not. He surveyed the throng with piercing eye as he
turned deliberately so as to face all sides of the great lodge.
He was at a loss for what to say. The call did not come again.
No one moved. No one spoke. There was silence in the throng.

The elder sister rose from her seat at the council, her clear
strong voice invading the awful silence in the lodge.

"See. Go out and see. Someone from another tribe may be
in need of help. You young men go. Go out and see!"

She immediately turned to the mothers and the older people
and entreated them to keep all the children indoors.

"The howl of Qwha-yha-tseek, the wolf, we know and
understand. This call that came from nowhere we know not
what it means. Take no more chances I say. Stay inside the
lodge and be safe."

The call did not come again. All the young men were appre-
hensive, that was evident as they looked at each other and
then to their senior, the old man with the black cane. The old
man, the master of ceremonies, would not commit himself.
He avoided their searching eyes for instruction or explanation.
The fires refused to draw and sputtered, emitting blue smoke
which did not rise but permeated the dank air inside the
lodge. The old man ventured to the great doors and reluctantly
stepped out. Immediately the young men followed after him
as did the rest of the menfolk and the older women who had
no charges on their hands.

In the sky to the east the blood was fading to a sickly yellow.
Sea-gulls wheeled high, high up in the sky, their white wings

reflecting the disturbed morning light when they made their tight circles. There was no wind now but a decided warm smell pervaded the morning air. There were no clouds visible in the sky. The sun came heavily over the craggy mountain to the east, it appeared dull and cold.

The river that had been placid and serene, its waters moving down gently intent in its search for the salt-chuck, now became murky. Early morning mist was wreathing, twisting and rising from its surface until it was completely enshrouded with the cold grey fog. Sea-gulls wheeled higher and higher into the heavens until they lost themselves out of sight of man.

No one had bothered to build the fires in front of the lodge. The air was cold, dank, foreboding. A shiver was felt through the crowd. The tide in the river was out. There was no visible life on its entire surface except for the eerie snaky mist that seemed to heave the already heavy mantle of fog higher up until it shrouded the bare tall maples across the river.

A lone dejected heap of a figure sat on the extreme brink of the river bank facing downstream. It was a woman — an old, old woman. She had her rain cape draped heavily over her slender shoulders and her rain hat, which came up to a sharp cone, clamped her head down and created the heap that was her. She moved not, nor did she speak. She just sat there facing downstream. Doing nothing.

There was a perceptible breeze. It moved across the river from the other side and nudged the heavy fog across and onto the bank where the lonely figure sat, so very alone, facing down the river. No one gave the figure any special attention after their first glimpse of her. The fog climbed the bank and swallowed her forlorn heap into its sinuous and ghostly mist. She was gone.

Whoo-whyyyyyyy!   Whoo-whyyyyyyy!

That heart-rending call again. Somewhere from the mist it came.

Whoo-whyyyyyyy!   Whoo-whyyyyyyy!

The call was faint. Did it issue from the mist? Did it come from the earth? Was it the voice of the wind from the north?

The old man with the black cane would not commit himself. He avoided the searching eyes of the young men and the now frightened women who nevertheless stole gradually towards the brink of the river bank. The call did not repeat after the fourth one.

There was a sand-bar some distance from the near bank of the river with a bit of water that ran downstream between it and the shore where the people stood gazing, bidding the sluggish sun to burst forth and take the mist away from the river.

A small dog whimpered, drew its tail between its hind legs and, shivering with fright, sought refuge between its master's legs. Nevertheless, it fixed timid eyes downstream, waiting. There was no sound. There was nothing. The call did not come again. The small dog slumped down, its head resting timidly on its forepaws, gazing unblinking downstream.

A faint imperceptible disturbance in the water was felt and seemed to come from downstream. Or was it the voice of the wind from the north that did not come with the morn? The old man would not relent. He avoided all eyes that sought his.

A dark patch evolved within the mist downstream and a figure, huge in the fog, gradually took shape into an over-sized human form. He wore over his broad shoulders a rain cape that flapped in the dark mist and upon his head there was a rain hat that came to a sharp cone at the crown. He waded in the shallow waters towards the sand-bar some distance from the shore where the people stood; they uncertain whether to run indoors and seek refuge around the fires, or to stay and learn what this thing was....

Whoo-whyyyyyyy!

The man-thing ripped off his rain cape and heaved it back into the mist. He grabbed at his rain hat and sent it sailing high up into the air. The hat skimmed aloft turning and rolling

97

because of its brim until it caught the reflection of the rays of the morning sun and was swallowed up in the grey fog.

Mist, the cold steam from the frigid waters enveloped the man-thing, and from the mist there came the fearful call again amid the turmoil of churning waters as the thing plunged into the icy void. There was silence. For a long time there was silence. The people peered into the dark misty fog of the early morn.

Whoo-whyyyyyyy!

That fearsome blood-curdling call burst forth without restraint. From a wild spray of boiling waters directly in front of the crowd, who were now huddled in a tight knot, it exploded. The man-thing leapt completely out of the waters. Straight upright he shot forth, his head, his chin, thrust upwards to reach a little higher. He disappeared back into the frigid waters at the same spot from where he had exploded so violently.

The small dog on the bank whimpered and abandoned his master, slinking into the open doors of the lodge. There was silence. The waters became calm again. There was no more movement in the waters.

HHHHHHHhhhhhhh. . . .

HHHHHHHhhhhhhh. . . .

The man-thing was out again. But this time he remained in the water treading mightily with his legs. His arms were held high above his head and in his strong large hands he clutched a small white dog. He held it aloft for a long moment before he disappeared under the misty waters for the third time, but reappeared immediately and remained in the water again holding the small defenceless dog in his large strong hands. He was still treading water mightily, his bare chest staying above the waters.

HHHHHHHhhhhhhh. . . .

HHHHHHHhhhhhhh. . . .

He shot straight out of the cold misty waters, the small dog still in his clutches. Then like a flash he pulled his arms violently downwards and pulled the white dog into his snarling mouth and tore it asunder with his fangs, the poor defenceless animal's blood spilling down his crazed countenance and dripping on to his bare chest.

HHHHHHHhhhhhhh. . . .

The man-thing thrashed back into the murky waters of the river. The fog thickened with the rising of the temperature above the waters. People stood as if rooted to their own spots and peered into the waters where the man-thing had disappeared leaving a red splotch in the clear waters of the river and a small patch of foam surrounded by ever widening rings of wavelets until they reached and were stopped by the sandbar. Another breath of air from across the river nudged the heavy fog up to and above the bank of the river where the people stood. From afar, a long way down the river, a faint call could be felt that bristled the hair behind the ears.

Whoo-whyyyyyyy.   Whoo-whyyyyyyy.

The sun loomed above the low grey fog that hung above the cold river. It was red. It rose heavily, the evaporating mist still snatching upwards as if to pull it down out of sight.

A scraggy naked limb of a dead maple across the river loomed out of the mist with clutching dead fingers. The struggling red disc rose into and labored past the clutching fingers of the dead limb which was naked and white, devoid of all covering.

The sun was out. It shone well above the horizon, big and strong. The mist that wreathed up from the surface of the cold river melted into the sunlight; the grey fog lifted and was gone; there on the brink of the river bank sat a lone figure facing downstream. On its slender shoulders there was draped a rain cape and upon its head there was a rain hat that went to a sharp cone at the crown.

A warm breath of air blew in from down the river. The people followed the old man as he went inside the great lodge shivering from the cold penetrating morning fog.

The fires inside were a welcome sight. They blazed energetically, red hot coals sizzling from large chunks of whale fat that had been fed to them, creating broad flames licking upwards. The people resumed their seats without direction or help from the ushers, glad to get back indoors to sit again beside warm fires. Children asked their mothers in timid voices, "What kept the people outside so long?"

It was quite late in the morning when the people came back indoors from the terrifying spectacle in the river. No one was inclined to speak of it or to discuss the meaning of it, if indeed there was a meaning. The old man still avoided the searching eyes that persistently sought his for an explanation, however brief it might be.

A sumptuous feast was being served, with no formal announcement from the hosts. Long stakes of cedar were being taken off the racks that were near the blazing fire. Pierced by the stakes were dried smoked clams that were prepared for this great Tloo-qwah-nah only a few weeks before and were still relatively fresh, their strong peculiar odor permeating the warm air inside the lodge.

Young men were busy serving, placing long impaled rows of smoked clams in front of the families while the womenfolk filled the waiting clam-shells with golden clear seal oil to dip their clams into for richer taste. The coastal tribes liked that. It was a staple that they enjoyed at home most frequently.

There were more speeches from the guests but they were all short and mostly thanking the hosts for an appetizing meal. The women tried hard to start a sing-song but with little success. People were in no mood for frolicsome gaiety, nor for laughter. The meal progressed slowly. The spirits of guests and hosts alike remained low in spite of the warm meal.

When the meal was at an end the Mah-moot, the left-over, was taken to the houses for the guests and for the hosts alike. The young men returned from their chores and were now sitting down eating at one end of the lodge. The children with their stomachs full were now climbing onto their mothers' laps and caressing them because they were happy again from the big meal.

It was tabu for new initiates to the Tloo-qwah-nah Society to eat certain foods for a period of time and clams were one of them. Accordingly the ten children who had been abducted by the wolves were given something else more appropriate for them at this time.

The long, long cedar mats that served as tablecloths were carefully swept off with switches made from hemlock branches whose thick and fine sprigs served well for this purpose. The mats were rolled up ready to be put away by the team of young men who had been doing their assigned duties during the entire event so well. The girls and unmarried young women sat prim and proper with their aunts or mothers because, it was believed, that at their particular age they were tender, sweet, attractive. They were the Us-mah, the revered ones, and so must remain coy, obedient. To be served, not serve, was their happy lot at that age. Indeed this was a crucial period that would mould their future lives when they would be on their own with families of their own to raise and manage.

"There is a lot of good in every man. This is our teaching. We believe it, you and I. We do our best to set the example for the young to see, to observe and to follow if it be in their hearts to do so. It is said that the child will grow up to be like father, like mother, like aunt, like uncle, because these people are nearest and thus dearest to him during his growing period.

"Moreover, moreover, to children these are the most important people in their lives; these are the people they will most likely want to be like when they grow to be men and women.

"It is so, a child is the shadow, the image, the reflection of the father, the mother, the aunt, the uncle. Thus our teachings, our tenets require of us to set a good responsible example, not only when we gather together as now when all eyes are cast in our direction, but on all occasions during the entire growing period of the child.

"It is said that one cannot deceive a child. It is said that he will grow up to be like those he has observed during his growing period. Thus is it no use to be good, to be generous, to be patient only when the eyes of people are cast upon you — you must be all these things and more when your own child's eye is cast upon you.

"To the mothers here in this lodge we give thanks. We thank you. This House is proud to have women of your stature, of your insight, of your compassion, because it is evident, it is evident that our tenets have been followed, the example that is good has been set. It is, it is shown through the cardinal virtues and behavior of all the children present. To the mothers we say, Tlah-coh, thank you.

"There is also evil. There are bad things, undesirable things. For these we must be, you and I, ever on the alert to recognize and reject, and not embrace, because they are different from that which is shown us by our loved ones and our elders who are our teachers. Evil appears in many different ways and manners.

"This morning, this morning we saw, we witnessed, perhaps one of the worst forms of evil. There is no need to stress this point. What we thought we saw this morning was not a desirable thing; not a thing to aspire to. What we thought we saw this morning was not for children to see. Different? True. It was different — it was spectacular.

"It was also not natural. It belongs to a world that is not ours. It belongs to a world that rejects the teachings of kindliness, compassion, consideration and love of nature and her children, be they big, strong, small or weak. It belongs to a world that delights in destruction in a cruel inhuman manner. It belongs to a world that turns its back to our Maker and Protector who made all nature and who dwells in all nature, including mankind. It is not for me to say, Don't do this, don't do that, but young men, it is for you to heed the voice that is in you. It is for you to say, that which I thought I saw in the morn with mine own eyes is not good, cannot be good. I will turn my back to it.

"It is not for me to tell you how to think. <u>Young men, you must your mind make up for yourself</u>."

THE BEAST IN MAN

From out of the waters it came with a moan.
Was it an animal?   Was it a man?
Alone it came for no other would condescend
To be its foe and not a friend.

You saw it gnash a dog in twain,
You saw the gore spill down the chin
While it the water trod.
You saw a grisly sight driven deep within the mind.

In the black waters of our lore
You saw a savage, a savage to the core.
The evil that you saw in the mist of the morn —
It was the beast in man.

The old man with the black cane was solemn and grave. He was more angry than sad when he at last interpreted the ghastly sight that had occurred early that morning in the waters of the river. He had begun his talk informally while he sat at ease near the fire that was next to the young men who were still eating their meal. His voice remained low and the note of sadness often crept in when anger was most expected of him. He spoke to no one in particular. He sought the earthen floor with his eyes, when he looked up it was the waning fire that his eye sought. His cane that was the symbol of his office lay inert upon his knees.

He spoke without authority. His was not the voice of experience. He was a man who saw an experience out there in the morn. He was merely repeating, to no one in particular, perhaps to himself, the reaction he felt within himself. He was one, he was part of the young men who sat and listened with great intent, straining their ears to catch every word that was uttered. No one moved. No one spoke. There was silence in the throng.

The young men who had seen the spectacle outside the lodge that morning listened most attentively. It was never said that the gory experience be a lesson for them. It was never said that it was the result of a teaching — or no teaching at all. It was understood and believed that because of their intense training from early childhood they would see and recognize that there was indeed evil therein.

It was evident that the old man with the black cane did not simply acquire his office as the master of ceremonies and interpreter for the House and the clan but that he merited the position by much work, with much preparation, with much thought and meditation in the hills and in the sanctuary of his sacred bathing pool deep within the wood. Long years of experience showed proudly upon his open countenance. He was old in seasons and yet, and yet, he could reach the young in thoughts that were uttered, perhaps to himself, perhaps to the fire.

The fires in the lodge waned on their hearths.

X

THE EVENTIDE OF THE DAY was creeping into the lodge. Black clouds had hidden the skies throughout the remainder of the day. No light seeped through the smoke-holes at the ridge of the roof. The wind outside was whining and whistling an eerie low tune in the outside corners of the great lodge.

The fires on their hearths were waning low, flickering and sputtering from their own coals. No one bothered to put a log upon the fire. There was a distinct chill in the air inside the lodge. It was awfully quiet outside save for the moaning of the wind from the north. "The wind has come back," some one declared, "we might have good weather again."

None of the young men who tended the fires could be seen. It was too quiet inside. The children slept peacefully in their mothers' arms, tired out from their long day in the lodge.

"There is evil. There are bad things, undesirable things."

The old man was repeating himself, perhaps, after all, he was growing a bit senile, perhaps his memory was waning like the fires upon their hearths, perhaps he was tired like the rest of the people. He drew up his stool which was made from the vertebra of a whale, its rich ivory color gleaming in the waning light of the fires, and edged closer to the warmth because of the chill in the air. His eyes, alive with thought, stared into the strong embers in the fire.

A stalwart brave so young, lithe of limb and willing too
Atracking down the elk would go
A quiver of arrows swung from shoulders, tendons strong
His trusty bow he would caress as he loped on through
Awending his way to the hills with a will
Amunching a chunk of fat smoked to his taste.

Ha!   The spoor was on the dew of the morn
The lope winds down into a stalk
Tloó-nim the elk he spies on a lofty crag
Beyond the line of spruce and pine
Up he lopes without delay
His heart is bold like the bow and twine.

Upon the flat, beyond the rock, he knows his quarry stands
Picks he the arrow so seldom used
The flint fits well the shaft
To the wind he circles fast, the mists embrace him now
The cutting wind, the creeping fog, he feels them not
For he is young, full of vigor and willing too.

Lord of the forest, he sees it now
Majestic, bold, it stands erect,
Great nostrils to the wind alert.
It sensed a danger but knew not where
Up he the weapon lifts, his bow so sure
The arrow pierces beneath the shoulder bone.

Alas!   The quarry is strong, it does not fall
To the summit and o'er the tor it crashes on
To stagger down the other side
Burdened sore with flint in the wound
Close its quarters he would remain
The hinds he must take home this night.

Down to timber-line it fights anew
As the hunter to its heels he drew
The red he tracks, it spills in spots
Tloó-nim the elk lingers then but not to stop
His spirits are high like the crown of the pine
His heart would sing with the bow and twine.

The hunter gathers speed to take the quarry now
Alas, Tloó-nim waxes stronger too
Down to forest, down to thickets, it stumbles strong

Down the valley it struggles with might and main
A stream it finds and plunges in, there to chill,
Congeal, the bleeding wound.

Down or up the stream?   Where has the quarry gone?
Tloó-nim, lord of the forest, has he lost?
Down the stream sped he without delay
Down to bog, to marsh and waste,
Through the moor, hard by a lake he canters still
Determined now, the elk he will take home.

He tarries, a drink to take from a pool of the lake
He lifts an eye, a bearing to take
The sun has sunk beyond the dell
Deep into the bowels of the forest still
Abiding not, as he was schooled
He straightway girds his loins right taut.

Make haste he must
In the slough it darkens fast
His heart is strong, he strides with might
As he rushes through the willowed heath
The lores of wise elders are soon forgotten
In his haste for to dash the forest through.

How long he has run he cannot say.   He stumbles now
        without heed
He is bruised, he is weary, he is beaten, he is spent,
He is hungry, water is a need
His feet are sore, cut deep with wound
His head it reels, no more will heed
He sinks beneath the bole of a cedar tree.

The sun has come and is gone again
Twice, yea three times, he sees this done
The precious fat?   There is no more
His lips will dry and crack for sure
His feet grow weary with blood, his own
And yet he sees no sight of home.

The moon has come and is gone again
Yet will he stagger on and on
The desire now is to last out
Tloó-nim the elk no longer is the meed
The salal green it gives him agony
The hemlock bark it sears him through and through

He sweats no more, fatigue will surely come
His hunger gone, the thirst will subside
Now the will is to stem his ebbing mind
So near to death, but will not die
He lingers now beneath the pine
A mist creeps fast into the eye.

One starless night he lay him down
Beneath the bole of a mighty pine
The night is still, there is no sound
A great silence chokes the forest line
His lips have healed and burn no more
His feet are tough, no longer sore.

Hark!   A whisper in the night
A word uttered in the wilderness tide
A murmur in the vast silence of the wild.
The omen rings so clearly into his mind
The torment now is deep within his thought
He has gone full wild to run the forest through.

The voice grows loud and stronger still
As he cowers in the moss and salal grille
Can he shake the mist that gathers in his eye?
The voice mocks now, like thunder in his mind
Straight from the bole of the mighty pine
And all things green in the weald.

Up he bounds with a mighty leap
The mocking grille no refuge would give
Too late now to recall the dangers of violent haste
To tarry long when doubts assail
Too late now to see the wisdom to abide
To use the lore bestowed by sires long ago.

To sleep secure if the mist to his eye should veil
Never to drink when on the canter or the chase
To save a morsel of the fat to slake the thirst if doubts assail
To search and climb the balsam tall
To sip its life-sustaining blood while he the region eyes
Instead of charging forth to run the forest through.

Too late now to recall instructions that were old
Should he find that he is lost in the forest wild
If his head should reel or the mist becloud the mind.
"Seek for, my son, the clump of bush, the only living growth

That will not whisper nor deride you through and through
Find the Cinnamox* bush to sleep within its restful bough."

"Heed the tenets of your people," an uncle would admonish.
How he scoffed, derided too, the counsels of his elders!
The weak get lost, he would jeer.   He could run the
    forest wall.
He was strong, he was young with heart stout and bold
That sang in tune with his bow so true
No one, he would boast, could tell him what to do.

Now the fear of death assailed him through and through
Yet still he stood aloof from the Protector true.
Creator of all mankind and all things too
Of the greens that e'en now would whisper in his mind
From the pine, the fir, the cedar tall in the wood
From all things green they whispered with refrain.

A man is lost, he will not die
He lingers now beneath the pine
His spirit took leave no more to live
In the body that tarries now to deny
The peaceful solitude of death sublime
On earth to roam for evermore.

The body is gaunt, all torments are lost
His hair grows hoary like the autumn night frost
The hue is misty, blue-green is the night
He is strong like the elk he would chase
But the spirit took flight to regions unknown.

In his quest, his hunger to halt
The knee will bend his back to stoop
His reason took wing, the eye will bulge out
As he peers into night for intrusion of man
The mind wanders now but linger he will
In the shadows of home he knew so well.

The voice that was his will fail him now
But his organ of smell will sharpen anew
The toes will vanish, his feet will club
Like the beast in the forest he would chase
His gait he has lost, now he shuffles forsooth
As he moves here and there in search of his meat.

*Blueberry.

He searches the pools of ebbing tide
For sculpins and bullheads that fill the belly now
He searches for greens, the cow-parsnip, at night
The rot of conky-wood may stay the hunger too
A look to the left, a peer to the right
He shuffles and shuffles with arms akimbo tight.

His speed increases like the wind in the night
He hides into rock, into earth out of sight
The bole of the pine will protect him now
He will prowl, he will hide, he will shy the daylight
And will whisper like greens in the night, Pook. Pook.
    Pook!
As he shuffles with arms akimbo tight, Pook. Pook. Pook!

The old man, with the black cane lying inert across his knees, was completely lost in his reverie as he related this legend of ancient lore. His eyes stared on the dying embers in the fire of the lodge. He spoke no more.

The young men and the throng were no longer watching the old man though they listened and heard every word that he uttered in his low and distant voice.

All eyes were now fixed on a strange eerie apparition that had manifested itself as if from nowhere. It was moving and shuffling hither and yon in the darkening shadows on the earthen floor. Someone said it appeared from the huge pillar beside the door. Others said it appeared from nowhere at all.

The thing was there. It was alive. It was a thing with human form. It was gaunt beyond belief. His face was cold, sad, devoid of feeling. The color, the hue of his skin was like the mist of a winter's night. There was no mirth. No life showed in his sunken eye. He was sad.

He shuffled along the earthen floor flitting hither and yon. His eerie shadow moved upon the cedar-plank wall of the lodge. The onlookers saw fresh snow upon his hoary head and his shoulders too. It did not melt because the body was cold. He moved, he shuffled with his arms tight akimbo. He peered through the openings of each arm. Though he moved with a shuffle he moved with uncanny speed. He seemed to move with no effort on his part. No patter of feet was heard on the earthen floor. He moved with silence.

Tied to the back of his head there was a small green twig — it stood straight up. From the end of this there dangled a twine with a fluffy white feather attached. Each move of his head made the feather bobble and dance, creating a pleasing effect in the darkening hall of the lodge.

The man-thing began to shuffle in a space between two fires. He stopped frequently in his stooping stance to peer through each arm. He was ever alert for the intrusion of man. Presently from his stooping mien he straightened to fling his head backwards with a jerk, spinning the white feather. Was he playing? Could he think? No one spoke. No one moved. There was silence in the throng.

The fire next to the door was dying out. It lay on its hearth in large glowing embers separated one from the other, bursting now and then in a garish blue flame.

The man-thing stopped abruptly in his shuffle. He bent forward low to peer through the hole made by his arm. He sensed something wrong. He was alert. There was no trust. Thus he stood perfectly still — listening, listening, listening. The fluffy white feather hung limply in front of him above the earthen floor. No one spoke. No one moved. There was silence everywhere.

A large ember that glowed with an eerie and weird color exploded, erupting a cloud of gray smoke, then sputtered and died. An involuntary, Ahhhh, escaped from one of the women.

The man-thing was not there. He was gone.

In his stead there was a sound of water — drip, drip, drip. Large drops of water were dripping on the hearth from the smoke-hole onto the smouldering dying embers. There was a chill in the atmosphere of the lodge.

> Perhaps within the dark recess of the mind
> There be a faint recollection of its kind
> When it sallies forth in the morn and the twilight.

A hint of frolic, a flutter of a play is apparent,
The shuffle, the nod, a murmur of a thought.
Perhaps there is hope — perhaps there is life within
    its breast?

The throng went home that night with thoughts deep within their own breasts, clutching their robes tightly around their shoulders, and into the first snow of the Moon of Little Sister.

XI

THE MORNING DAWNED BRIGHT AND BEAUTIFUL. There was some snow on the ground but not too much. After the last two gruelling days the people were given a respite and allowed to sleep late. In fact it was noon when the village crier gave forth his lusty call.

"Walk now at once! Let not your king in his lodge sit alone."

The teams of young men had cleaned the front of the great lodge and its immense roof of snow in the early hours of the morning, the wood pile inside was replenished and all the guests' great canoes were cleaned of snow and covered again with their protective cedar mats. Blue smoke issued forth from the smoke-holes on the ridge of the lodge while steam from the melting snow rose sluggishly from the cedar-plank roof as the morning sun smiled down.

All the councillors were in their seats when the first guests arrived and as they entered, the sweet appetizing aroma of roasting elk meat greeted them from the many slanting racks that encircled the great fires, warming the meat that had been pre-roasted and half-smoked some time before.

The guests took their own seats with no time lost. The young men rolled out the long cedar mat table-cloths and another feast was in progress. The meat was taken off the racks and placed directly onto the cedar mats while the younger men set brimming large oil dishes before each family to dip their elk meat in.

There were many complimentary remarks about the elk meat feast with the bounteous supply of seal oil and also about the chunks of smoked fur-seal blubber that were tied neatly with phi-tsoop, strands of the inner red cedar bark. The older men enjoyed biting chunks of this blubber between mouthfuls of elk meat. A festive board, not easily surpassed, it was said.

True to the festive spirit of the day the womenfolk began a lively sing-song with the younger ones doing the Chees-chees-suh, the Dance of Gladness. Everyone was in a jovial mood again. More and more menfolk joined in on the side, drumming or simply clapping their hands in time with the beat of each song.

HHHHOOOO-HO HO HO HO HO.   Hoy.   Hoy.

The loudest howl-call came from outside. It drowned out the entire sing-song, thunder-drums and all.

HHHHOOOO-HO HO HO HO HO.   Hoy.   Hoy.

With a clatter and a roar, upsetting all things that got in his way, the largest man imaginable bull-dozed his way into the lodge. He did not rush in, but picked his way as he pushed and toppled everything within reach and repeated his ear-splitting howl, turning round and round all the while, moving ponderously as he approached the people and showing his enormous back most of the time. Every few deliberate steps he would peer down to the earthen floor as if to plot and ascertain which way to move next. He had enormous feet, and hands enormous beyond belief that were blackened with the war-black paint. When he reached the light of fires and turned to face the women's and children's section he showed an enormous and most grotesque face. His eyes were black and extremely small, his nose was huge, hooked and hawklike and jutted out from beneath bushy black eyebrows. The mouth was small and round expressing the howl that he emitted so vociferously and at frequent intervals. One cheek was considerably lower than the other and there was no chin. The huge man wore a mask — a mask carved from the bole of the yellow cedar tree. He was the Yellow Cedar Face. The spirit of yellow cedar.

The huge man was groping his way along the earthen floor again. With his right hand he would feel the air with palm forward and draw it back to his nostrils. He was smelling his way instead of seeing. Thus he wandered around the great lodge feeling, peering, plotting and howling his huge person slowly hither and yon. He seemed to be in search of something because at times he showed some excitement while at other times with his smelling advance he by-passed areas that he found himself near.

He was now near the area where the young men sat and he visibly became more agitated in his heaving about. He began pushing things down and destroying them with his enormous feet. He had now come to the area of the young men and he emitted a howl that would split eardrums as he blindly charged forward, upsetting great cedar boxes and hurling them to the middle of the earthen floor, pushing down posts behind fleeing men, amid the screams of little children as they cowered into their mothers' arms.

Immediately in front of him the area was open. The huge man stopped his advance abruptly, smelling and peering blindly forward. Directly in front of him there was a small door. It was painted a garish orange-red. After a prolonged peer towards it he seemed to have espied it for with a howl, even louder than his last, he groped forward until he was within a few inches of the bright colored door, peering and staring at it for a long moment. It was evident that he had found what he was searching for. Slowly, painfully, his own find seemed to register in his mind. He began to heave up and down, his great grotesque mask heaving with his motions as if to comply with a remote thought. . . . This is it.

HHHHOOOOOOOOOOOOOO. With a mighty howl he stretched forth one arm and with his enormous hand he grabbed the door and tore it off its hinges. He flung it to the

Yellow Cedar Face

floor under him and stomped on it with his great feet. The new door broke and splintered into many pieces as he passed over it to pull down the studs and sagging lintel. He heaved his way into the small room that the door had hidden and with yet another howl he reappeared.

In his huge hand he grasped a chamber, hewn from the bole of some wood. He flung the chamber to the earthen floor with such force that it broke into several pieces, but this did not appease his apparent anger for with howls that were frightening he stomped the fragments under his enormous feet, kicking and scattering the pieces about the floor. He was angry.

When there were no more pieces to trample his anger was also spent. He was appeased, or so it seemed, for he straightened up and began his peering and smelling advance once again. The huge creature found himself in an open space to the side of the end fires nearest to the children's area. He stopped to examine the earthen floor, peering down low in order to see, squinting and nodding his grotesque wooden face to one side then to the other. He was beating out a slow rhythm with his enormous head. Presently a faint oomb of the thunder-drum was heard from somewhere in the lodge and the big man began swaying from one side to the other, keeping time with the beat of the drum.

Children squealed with delight and hugged their mothers closer, encircling their small arms around their mothers' necks. The huge man seemed to sense the little ones' delight for he began to perform with all his might and with great gusto he heaved about most ponderously, turning every which way in order to be seen by all, stopping frequently to stoop down low and squint at the earthen floor to plot out his course.

Light from the fires showed that there were no sockets in the small squinting eyes, that the brows were extremely heavy and very broad. The nose was narrow and prodigiously hooked, showing no nostrils at all, the chin was sawed off directly below the howling mouth. In spite of the wooden face's extreme grotesqueness it seemed to manifest a sort of kindliness. When it peered and squinted towards the children, shifting its weight at an alarming angle without falling forward the children squealed again with glee and excitement.

It was apparent now that the big man was pacified. He did not utter any more of his ear-splitting howls and his movements were relatively docile. During one of his exploratory squints to the earthen floor so that he might advance forward he slowly and painfully seemed to make out a foot that was directly in front of his large nose. Very slowly and very deliberately he surveyed the hazy and beclouded object, squinting and tilting his large head from side to side.

Slowly his gaze moved up to the knee, the lap, the torso, the breast, and finally to the long hair of the woman whose foot he had discovered. With much labored scrutiny it seemed to steal into his brain that the object of his intense study was a female. Forthwith the oversized muscular man with the prodigious face became the king of all lovers. He was every bit as charming as the Son of Mink, the lover of all the animal world.

He pawed and he fondled the poor frightened woman with his enormous hands, stroking and parting her hair until he was so carried away with her beauty that he actually clambered up on her lap, to the screaming delight of the children, as he squinted and peered into the face of the terrified woman, his own wooden face inches away from hers.

Presently four brave men, each with a rattle in hand, cautiously approached the erstwhile lover and somehow induced him to desist. After some persuasion the big man was rattled out of the lodge amid a great hush from the throng for fear that he might howl again.

"Mother, will he come again?" a small eager voice was heard to ask.

A tale is told of long ago:
All things, it is said, must come and go,
All things, it is said, have a spirit,
The moss, the bracken, the tree with a bole.
To your lodge, with no warning, it will come.
Shun him not but make room for his welcome.

A howling clamorous rogue from the wood,
Over all braves he towers with manhood.
His arms are long like the limb of the cedar;
His legs are strong and full of power;
His feet are big, his weight to sustain;
His hands, enormous for might and main.

It is said, he a mission must maintain
For men of our clan and also your own,
When still they are young and growing with strength.
For a vessel he seeks that he must unearth.
No man with pride and dignity true
Inside a house, this vessel should use.

Should the vessel he seeks, it is said
Be kept in a lodge or in a shed,
A visit from him will be made forthright
With a voice that is skookum[1] with might.
No pillars, no doors, will stay his wrath
Till the kiss-duh[2] he seeks he does unearth.

Make room, it is said and anger him not
He will to the clootchmen[3] stay coy
Make room for him, for rare is the chance
To witness him, for the children dance.
He is big, he is strong without a doubt
But he is kind, big-hearted to a fault.

Yea, his back is strong like the cedar tall
But his mind is slow feeble and dull.
The sense of his smell is keen — acute
But bleary the eye and weak is the sight.
Strong and skookum is the howl.
A spirit with a mask of a cedar bole.

[1] Powerful.
[2] Chamber-pot.
[3] Wives.

XII

THE MOON OF LITTLE SISTER marked the winter season. Cold winds from the north brought the snow, the frost that turned into ice in the night to shine and sparkle when the sun came out in the morning. It grew cold when the Moon of Little Sister came.

Ahhh! Little Sister brought with her other things that were good.

Kí-tla-noose, the fur-seal — one of the most sought after Ahh-toop, sea-water game, for its beautiful fur, its meat and its life-giving oils — came inshore with the coming of the Moon of Little Sister to rest awhile from its long migration from the north to milder climes farther south. It would gambol and play, sailing with its black flipper raised high in the air to catch the wind from the north in the inland waters of these people. It waved and beckoned, as it were, to the hunter to come and take it, if he could.

A small party of seal-hunters had gone down to the sound to meet the arrival of the first kí-tla-noose. Now they were back, four canoes in all. They came up the river with the incoming tide under cover of darkness as was their wont. The watchman of the night had awakened the clan who now stood silently on the beach, ready with their skinning and slicing knives. The sealing canoes slid in silently. Stern first they came in to be eased up onto the grassy beach by strong willing hands. Each craft was loaded to the limit for fast travel and for safety. Forty miles twice they had gone for this prize. It was all of forty miles one way to the inland fur-seal banks. The last carcass that was cut, skinned, sliced and brought into the lodge made the number Ah-tleek, an even forty.

The morning dawned cold but dry. The sun rose over the arête to the east bold and strong. Wind from the north blew the hoarfrost off the naked trees, sparkling and shimmering against the rising sun.

Crows came in flocks with their scolding talk. Qwin-eé, the sea-gulls, screamed them away, to peck and clean the place on the beach before the mink packed the offal away.

Guests and hosts alike entered the lodge with vast smiles upon their countenances. The aroma of the meat was sweet to smell. It permeated the air inside and outside the lodge. It was good.

The head cook was busy and the old man with the black cane was overseeing the great roast. Massive carcasses were impaled on sturdy poles that rested on stout limbs driven into the earthen floor and were roasting all around the four fires. Great racks up above held long strips of meat and the fat, roasting and smoking them too.

> He-oh he-oh, said the voice of common assent,
> We see now what a great House you are
> Day by day we come to your lodge with deep awe
> We wonder and ponder what will come next.

> The Qwah-niss[1] came when there was none to be had
> Hi-chin, the clam, our palates did please
> Tloó-nim, the elk, whose meat we enjoyed
> Chims, the black bear, provided your oil.

> We know the meat that is made in the Moon of
>   Salmonberry[2]
> We make the same for our winter store
> Here now we sit agog delighted to see
> This Kí-tla-noose[3] that is fresh from the sea.

1 Camas bulb.
2 In the month of May.
3 Fur-seal.

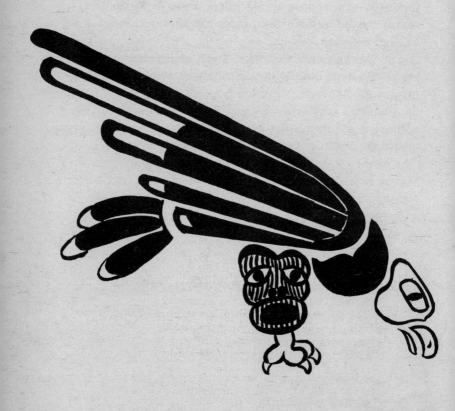

A Great Thunderbird

Ahh-aye   Ahh-aye.   So be it.   So be it.
It is true you with your clans make this House
It stands noble and strong in the Ten Alliance.
Tlah-coh, many thanks, we do offer from our clan.

It was an informal address of gratitude made by the speaker
with the soft speaking voice. He gave the speech while he sat
amongst his own clan. All the other speakers knew and understood that he spoke for the nine other tribes that were in the
lodge. No other speaker rose. Now it was time for a rest in
the warm atmosphere of the lodge. Time to sit and relax,
stretch the limbs and loll about while the meat roasted all
around the great fires.

The old man with the black cane, and his low stool that
was made from the vertebra of a whale, moved to the children's section. Slowly, deliberately he set his legless seat down
on the earthen floor. There was a broad smile upon his kindly,
wizened face. The children gathered close around for they
loved him dearly.

A long time ago when yet young and strong
To a great Tloo-qwah-nah we went with a song
The people to the north do sing with vigor
They dance too with beauty and with grace.

Ornate rattles purled loud for their rites
While our hosts displayed their To-pah-ti[1]
Many a play was offered with great fun
The songs were sung with loud thunder-drums.

Festive games, their To-pah-ti, are hard to surpass
We were to discover with great surprise
We marvelled at plays that were shown
That left us bewildered with artful illusions.

A great thunderbird sat on Ni-toop the beam
Its great imposing beak was all aglow
With eyes that were huge to see through the dark
With slats of cedar bark its body was made.

[1] Festive games or mystical inherited rites.

The wings were long for strength and power
They were hewn from the cedar shake
White tail-feathers fastened tight with thongs
Thunderbird looked big and skookum too.

Moving not, there it sat all day all night
Staring, glaring down with an ominous eye
At Mah-uk the whale that was near the wall
Unmoving too it rested on the earthen floor.

Through the long ceremonials of the winter moon
The bird sat on the beam with talons strong
Mah-uk too by the door had no life
It was hewn from the bole of a cedar tree.

The night was calm, there was no wind
A man from the shadows rose rattle in hand
He rendered his runes that were weird
Observing the four corners of the lodge.

The incantations done he remained upright
Gazing to'ards the door with eyes intent
The rattle in his hand rolled forth anew
He stood tall with unblushing mien.

Loud and louder still the rattle purled
His eye fixed on the door's cedar sill
His voice now mute, no one else moved
The fire flickered at the other end.

To blaze with a glow all its own,
For it was fed with pine tree cones,
Now lending its light to a darkening hall
As the fire waxed strong for awhile.

Lo and behold! from under the sill
Ah-mah the loon appeared, brazen and bold.
From cedar wood adzed, seasoned and black
An adornment of white encircling the neck.

With beak held high it moved down the aisle
Invading the silence with its piercing call
Echoing now against the cedar plank wall
Rising to the ridge and through the smoke-hole.

Four times it gave the wilderness call
How proudly it bore itself down the aisle!
At the far end to vanish into the floor
Ah-mah had come from a mountain pool.

Still another man with sacred rattle sound
A chant that was solemn and grave
Stood forth before the crowd in the hall.
How proudly he held himself before the throng!

To four sides of the lodge turned he with grim face
Weird was the chant that went forth for awhile
Rising now with power to the beams proud and aloof
Only to wane and die within the vaulted hall.

The chant was stilled now.   His voice was mute.
With gathering strength the rattle purled
From hand to beam it soared around the hall
To settle again into his waiting palm.

Many magic skills were shown that night
Which baffled us all without a doubt
To-pah-ti, their arts, are hard to surpass
This we now know with much surprise.

The thunderbird sat on Ni-toop[1] in the lodge
Grasping the beam with his talons strong
Glaring down with an eye that saw nought.
The eye was made from a cedar knot.

One stormy night rain and hail pelted the roof
A quake shook the lodge from the earth to its ridge
Much fire and lightning flashed everywhere
Without reprieve, rending all silence asunder.

Mah-uk the whale on the earthen floor
With a great heigh and a great Ho!
Trembled a little, came to life with a heave
Spuming foam high with a mighty blow.

The thunderbird shook its body of cedar bark
Lifted pinions that were made from cedar planks
With cedar slat wings spread high for power
Down it swooped to'ards the earthen floor.

Amid rain and hail that pelted from the ridge
The bird settled on Mah-uk at the door
With talons strong he lifted with might
And carried the whale to his beam aloft.

[1] A beam.

To sit once more with bold glaring eyes
On Ni-toop, his talons grasping tight.
With eyes unblinking, unable to see
For they were made from a cedar knot.

The rains and the hail came no more in the lodge
When the bird settled itself aloft once more.
Much cedar wood was thrown on the fires now
Great were the sparks that burst forth aglow.

The man stood bold with the rattle in his hand
Tall and aloof with dignified pride.
Faint, so gentle, was the purl when it sounded
For his fame he had shown his To-pah-ti.

The people to the north do sing with vigor
Hah!   They do dance with beauty and with grace
Proudly sacred rattles purl for their rites
When they show their own festive games.

Their To-pah-ti, I say, are hard to surpass
This we conceded and with much surprise
As we marvelled at plays to us shown
That left us bewildered by their magic skills.

The children sat silent and awed by the tale of the old man.
They felt that he had lived a long, long time. He had captivated them completely with his soft, kindly voice and with his
quaint and pleasing demonstrations of the movements, sounds
or calls of his most unusual tales. The women, too, were fascinated as they held their children on their knees, grateful that
they were so well entertained while the meat was being roasted
for the great feast.

Fresh roasted meat from the big spits and the half-smoked
long strips from the racks were being lowered by the teams of
young men to be put into large feast dishes and placed before
the families. This was done with speed and great efficiency
acquired through long practice, good management and directions from the head cook and the old man with the black cane.

With this meat some more of the Qwah-niss, camas, was
served but this time cold and also a species of wild potato,

Koo-himtl, that was provided by a relative from a neighboring tribe. However, the guests ate these vegetables as a last course — thus treating them as a dessert.

Many speakers stood up to acknowledge the rare meat, to thank once again for another feast in their honor, each taking much time, each speaking with great wisdom and knowledge of intertribal ancestry.

This was a time to relax, stretch the limbs and take a breather. Every one was in high spirits, from the children, the young men, the womenfolk and so on to the honored guests and finally the hosts of this great Tloo-qwah-nah.

Many days had come and gone since its inception, there had been many extremely tense and dramatic moments throughout the entire affair for the word Tloo-qwah-nah meant when one stopped acting or emoting and began *living* the part.

Thus far all undertakings including the story-telling had been executed and rendered in the spirit of Tloo-qwah-nah. Now this opportunity to rest and be thankful was a welcome much needed respite for the onlookers, the guests, as well as for the hosts and authors of the great event.

This too was a time for the home tribe members to go home for awhile if they so wished to do chores at their own homes. During the meal many stories, experiences and tales were told informally to small groups of men, women and children while they ate. There was an audible hum throughout the great hall.

In accordance with long established custom the womenfolk rose to do the Dance of Gladness, drumming softly as they sang and performed the slow swaying movements of thank-offering. When one group finished another started until the dance was performed four times, one for each side of the lodge.

XIII

THE MORNING AND THE AFTERNOON WENT FAST. It had been cold, quiet closed-in weather. Leaden clouds had hung low all throughout the wintry day. A good time to stay indoors.

The Moon of Little Sister had bloomed to her full roundness. Now she was again struggling up and over the arête to the east. Later and later in the night she came from behind a heavy maze of mist and fog, losing shape for awhile, to gain again her beautiful crescent form. There was no moon on this evening to start another night, no shadows played outdoors to warn of the coming of night — daylight seemed to have simply turned to darkness.

The great hall was still humming with the low inaudible voices of the people when the old man with the black cane emerged from the councillor's section. The hum ceased instantly upon his appearance. He looked perfectly calm and at ease as he moved to the middle of the end of the great lodge. Facing first towards the councillors, thence around the hall he turned slowly to denote that his announcement would be for all and concern all present in the lodge. His black cane was in front of him, its extreme tip resting lightly on the floor, another indication that the forthcoming message was to be a formal one. Both his hands rested on top of the symbolic cane, one on top of the other, his head and face bowed towards the earthen floor. A gesture of self-humiliation for all speakers and announcers prior to the deliverance of a message.

Choo-why-tligh, choo-why-tligh,
Honored guests of all tribes, hear me now.
You will stay for awhile, comfort now the limb
At this time, good news it is that has come.

Hha-witl-ee, the head of this tribe
Does wish at this time to describe
The passion that has come to his heart,
Engendered by the joys as shown by all guests.

At the inception of this great gathering
It was said that he would stand and sing.
See now, his drums are warming by the fire,
The time has come to complete that desire.

For our people Ha-oomb is the staff of life.
At this time it is warming on the fire.
The water too is coming to a boil,
The coals are being stoked for the broil.

This head of our clans, to your ally belongs
With the Ten that make the people strong.
Hark now his voice and take his hand,
Share with him the abundance of his land.

Comfort now the limb, honored guests of all tribes.
This House will stand and sing with pride,
When the drum is sounded in his lodge
The Head will don the robes to show his badge.

Stand now, stand now young men of this House.
Clap your hand when you lift your voice.
The food, the staff of life for all our people
On the fire is warming for your pleasure.

The time is here to show his own ritual.
The time has come to sound the thunder-drum.
The time is now, to stand with him,
Lift, with your voice, the foundation of his house.

The senior men together with the young men of the tribe
stood one hundred strong in front of the Head's quarters, each
facing away from the throng. They made a human curtain

for what was to come. Thus they stood silent and with their heads bent, their eyes fixed on the earthen floor of the great lodge.

From behind this human curtain the old man with the black cane emerged and, without any preliminary gestures or preamble, in a strong voice bade the home people to stand now for the food was already on the fire.

"Stand now and give thanks to Him who provides!"

At the precise moment, on the down-beat of the song-leader's eagle white feather wand, the drums boomed forth — twenty in all.

One, two, three. One, two, three. The deep throated skin drums boomed out the beat for the grace, the thanksgiving song of the tribe.

Men, women and children stood tall on both feet. The home people and the guests alike stood up to give with a song their thanks to their Creator, Provider of All Wants.

One, two, three. One, two, three.

The song, the grace, started off with one voice to be joined by the one hundred strong and to swell with the voice of the throng. Well before the chorus was reached a voice — a full octave higher than the key used — directed, "The chorus. Sing the chorus next," intoning in the same high key the exact words to be used. Line by line as the chorus was being sung, with the same direction, the chorus was repeated and at the last verse the entire throng joined with so much heart that the foundations of the House were indeed lifted. The eagle feather wand was high, high in the air to swing down as the song ended with a mighty boom of the drums.

The home people and the guests sat down to their places and waited for the food that was to come, wondering and guessing what new food would be offered and served.

The great doors opened and the team of young men whose duty it was to serve during this Tloo-qwah-nah entered. Two men with great care carried large feast dishes or tubs that were steaming from the food they contained, a third young man followed behind to serve the meal into wooden platters and basins that were brought in by two other young men, making five in a team.

The human wall or curtain had remained standing, their backs still towards the throng. From behind this the song leader's voice was again heard, now intoning the opening lines of the song that was to be sung for whatever was yet to come. The song was slower in tempo but with a more intricate beat. The basic three beats were discernible but at frequent intervals it rambled to five faster beats in a row without a rest.

As the thunder-drums boomed forth the line of men that made the screen parted in the middle to display a mural for the king, a great thunderbird was predominant in the centre carrying in its talon Mah-uk, the whale, and superimposed on the top corners were the form of the wolf. These were the symbols of his House. The mural was original, showing the form, the bone structure and a discreet innard to balance the design that made the mural.

The song went the full length and ended on a long-drawn-out note. Again the song leader intoned the opening bars without a rest. Upon the boom of the drums, with the commencement of the first line, the great mural lowered to reveal a huge mask. It remained motionless as if suspended for it was screened off from the chin down with a black robe.

Slowly and almost imperceptibly it began to show movement. The mouth started to move and chomp up and down, the great eyes began to blink. Now it was alive, bobbing slightly and swaying with the slow rhythm of the song, the huge face lifting to the skies on the three distinct beats and inclining to the earth on the five successive beats. The song was sung the four full times to comply with the laws, long-standing throughout the entire coast.

The huge mural was raised again and the mask was hidden behind. There was a profound message inherent in the whole presentation — the bigness of the mask denoted the owner's magnitude and degree of influence, power and authority; the blinking and the rolling of the huge eyes told of the owner's will to watch over and look to the wants of his subjects; the chewing and the chomping of the mouth indicated, with no words, his ability to provide food for his people; the face lifting towards the skies and its subsequent bow to the earth told dramatically that the owner lifted his face to the heavens for strength while he, a mere earthling, remained rooted firmly to the earth to serve all who entered his domain. That was the message, these were the tenets for all the people of the coast.

Upon completion of the presentation the speaker, the tribe's historian, rose to recount in great detail the story, the legend and the meaning of the mural and its significance to the tribe. He spoke at length to the home people in general thanking them for the response that they had all made, for their regular attendance and for their actual participation in the feasts, the games, the plays and the numerous dances and sing-songs that had already taken place. With great diplomacy he outlined, he recounted and he reminded all those present in the lodge of the limits, the boundaries of the chief's domain and of the game, the creeping creatures of the land, the swimming and diving-under-sea water denizens, and the fowl of the air that migrated or stayed. All things within his boundaries belonged to him and his chiefs, protected with as much fervor and diligence as other such holdings. Tactfully, the speaker observed that without such principles and agreements feasts and Tloo-qwah-nah would be onerous indeed if not altogether impossible.

Relax and comfort your limbs, from the fire the food is out.
You have sung the song that makes the water hot.
The staff of life for our people is now ready.
Partake now, with good faith to make your mind steady.
'Tis the food that draws all people together
For all partake and enjoy where'er they may gather.

Eat now and be merry with our ruler,
The offering that is from his larder.
This represents a portion of his opulence.
He extends his hand to you in all reverence,
Take now the hand and share with him
The joy that is within him at this time.

The men who made the human screen dispersed, leaving the mural in full view for the throng to see and study if they were so inclined. The thunder-drums were put away near the fire to warm again. From the large feast-dishes the young men began to serve out the food onto wooden platters and basins that were provided. The food came steaming out of the large containers and from the ever expectant guests there was an audible, Hhoooooooo! Chooooooo! Choo, choo, choo, cho, cho cho! An expression common to all people of the coast for a complete and agreeable surprise. The food offered by the ruler of the tribe was winter spring salmon, the Soo-hah.

Broth in the feast-dishes was kept and served in wooden basins into which whole families dipped gleaming white clam-shells to sip the rich taste of the Soo-hah. Other men served sockeye, cohoe and summer spring salmon which had all been smoked and well dried in the summer and in the fall. For this course liberal quantities of the oil was provided and the guests partook of the oils liberally.

Unbeknown to the guests, and indeed to most of the home people, ten fishing canoes had journeyed down the inlet and so to the sea to fish and to troll for the winter spring salmon as they swarmed into the bays of the sound following great hordes of Kloos-mit, herring. In a few days the canoes had come back fully laden with the bright shining salmon.

All the salmon, cooked in boiling water, was done in another lodge so that the surprise would be complete. To the sea-dwelling guests it was indeed a surprise to eat winter spring salmon at these inland hills so far, far away from the sea. These were the first winter "springs" brought in and all the people of the confederacy shared alike according to their appetite — thus demonstrating, again without words, the whole purpose of the laws and customs of the coast.

The people ate well, so well indeed that very little was taken home for their Mah-moot,* to the delight of the hosts.

The speaker had continued with his oration during the course of the feast, the listeners swallowing the axioms and words of wisdom while they swallowed their food. He spoke slowly in a low soothing voice. The intent was to reach the people through each one's individual mind. This was not the time to rouse and excite. This was a time to woo for contentment.

> The Moon of Little Sister is waning in the heaven,
> Twenty plus six days have come and are gone again
> When the portals of this lodge were lifted for your clan
> Leaving us two more days in which to lower it again.
> Prouder and stronger still, this House has grown
> Because of your entry, participation therein.
>
> Honored guests from all the tribes
> This tribe is replete with your noble pride.
> The king of this House is glad for your acceptance
> To take his hand, his oils, the symbol of his affluence.
> Comfort the limb and sit again,
> He will sing you one more song.

Once again the men were assembled in the front making a screen with their bodies, standing close together. The thunder-drums were out, four on each end of the screen. Up there in the front, above the heads of the singers, the mural was imposing with its own bold relief against the dark back wall. The song that was sung to give thanks for the meal was sung again although the feast was not yet over and still must not be put away. On the second round of the song a dancer appeared from behind the human screen. He was a young man dressed in a black cape and upon his head there was the headdress of the sea-serpent.

*Left-overs.

He came into view with his headdress poised high, surveying the expanse of the imagined sea with its huge unblinking eye. He moved on the balls of his feet, gliding along the earthen floor. There was no chop or dip to his movements, he glided to simulate the sinuous, gliding movement of the sea-serpent upon the surface of the sea. Each movement, each step, was governed by the beat of the drums, his feet barely leaving the surface of the floor. One, two, three. One, two, three. The gaudy, bright-colored sea-serpent proudly eyed, proudly surveyed, his domain. Now reaching high towards the horizon, bold and imperious, to settle low again undulating as if with the sea as he turned gracefully at the end of the arena. When the song ended the dancer dropped to the floor at the precise moment of the last beat of the drum and darted behind the screen all in one flowing movement.

On the third round of the song the sea-serpent was livelier and when the song leader intoned the words of the chorus he seemed more alert, more expressive in his movements and when the chorus was reached he danced with renewed vigor, prancing, gyrating, moving next to the earthen floor on his haunches, ending the dance with a burst of whirls on his bended knees to dart behind on the last boom of the very loud drum. The song ended and came again with no rest for the dancer who was out again to repeat the last performance.

Fires waned low on their hearths, wood was not put on. It was time to go home. The ceremonial things were being put away for the night. The throng sat, reluctant to leave.

XIV

THE MOON OF LITTLE SISTER had come so proudly with her twin pointed crescent. She had waxed nightly till she rounded out to her full glory, to wane and vanish again in the morning sky with her twin pointed crescent a pale transparent sliver in the dawning western sky. Though the people would not see her now she hoped that she would see the end of this gathering of people whose common cause was, "To get to know each other."

It was a glorious night when the throng went home from the lodge. The stars in the heavens were shining and twinkling. The Milky Way seemed stronger, wider and brighter with the absence of the moon.

The short one, the youngest brother of the family who was sponsoring this Tloo-qwah-nah, was the last one to leave the great lodge. He was excited. He was impatient for the new day to come. It was to be their day. There was so much to be done and so little time left in which to do it. Time had flown by on the wings of the Moon of Little Sister. Now, for another season, she was gone.

The Short One found himself in his sacred shrine. With the light from the stars he had found the well-hidden path that led to this bathing place. He had already fulfilled the obligations to the tenets of his people. In his pool he had bathed, rubbing his body and carefully massaging his muscles with the sweet-smelling evergreens that were his family's delight. His quest was never for the sturdy stalwart frame. His desire was

Sea Serpent Dance

to be supple like the young sapling in the wood. To move with grace like Panta, the mountain lion.

He stood now, still and motionless against a young pine tree. His gaze was on the shimmering waters of a nearby tarn. He was intent in his attitude of listening. The impatience, the troubled feeling within his breast was gone. He had spoken to his Creator, his Provider of All Wants during his ablution only a moment ago.

It came. With the first hint of light on the placid waters of the tarn the call came. Clear and strong upon the morn it came shattering asunder the silence of the moonless night. The plaintive wilderness call of the loon shot across the narrow lake, echoed back from the steep mossy bluffs to ascend to the heavens, to be lost up there and not come back to earth.

Next to singing and dancing the Short One loved to sit and listen for the miracles of nature, to feel her silence in his very own soul. There was a time, much like this one, when he found, when he discovered, the lair of a mountain lion. As now, he had stood beneath a young pine when the first rays of morning light wedged through the dense forest to reveal the moss on the forest floor.

There before his eyes he espied a she lion feeding a pair of young where a shaft of sunbeam entered her lair's hidden entrance. As now, he had stood still, and watched the beautiful cat stretch and curl with the pulling of the robust growing kittens until the beam passed along and left the den in darkness once more. And now he had again heard the wilderness call that thrilled him through and through, lifting his own spirit to soar in the heavens in thoughts that were pure, beautiful and good.

The fires in the lodge were already blazing invitingly when the Short One returned from his night's vigil. Through the long winter's night he had cleansed his body while he talked to his God. The wilderness call of the loon had lifted his spirit to heights known only to those who seek and believe in the lofty ideals of total peace with one's own conscience.

Prior to all undertakings of importance it was expected of a man that he stand vigil all through the night and not sleep. The Short One needed no prompting in this regard because of his intense and deep-rooted convictions regarding long established tenets, particularly this one. Perhaps it was because of this that the Short One was prone to muse and think, to meditate in realms usually removed from other men; to see, to observe movements of a moody nature and interpret them in his dances; to sense and hear nature's ever-changing sounds and compose them into his songs, chants and croon-cadences — like the drone of the winds from the north in the estuary that he had heard and composed into a song not long ago.

By nature the Short One was a poet, a songmaker and a dancer. His repute was great in spite of his youth. In terms of seasons he was at the peak of his manhood — perhaps he had seen thirty plus five summers. Even now his songs were sung along the north-west coast as far north as the shores of Sitka in fair exchange for other songs from those regions, even now his dances were known and recognized as among the inimitable and he had performed from Quilleute south of the 49th parallel to the shores of Sitka in Alaska.

To him this occasion, this particular Tloo-qwah-nah meant, represented, something extraordinary. He had seen and participated in many like gatherings but somehow he felt, he sensed deep down within himself, that this would mean much more than just another Tloo-qwah-nah. He was determined to do his very best. He would, with his new song, The Wind, introduce the new dance that he had invented recently and had perfected with his younger "brother," his cousin. The new song would fit in perfectly with the other older songs, making an even array of ten songs. Yes, he would call them, Array of Ten Songs. He would sing all the songs without a stop. Ten songs. Different, he mused.

At this moment his "brother," his partner, came in and approached him immediately.

"I have been looking for you since last night. When you were nowhere to be found I knew that you had gone out. I was out myself and have just returned. This is our day?"

The Short One was a man of few words. His partner knew that and long before had stopped asking him pertinent questions. Patiently he waited for him to answer and perhaps brief him of his immediate plans. It was evident that the two young men were very close to each other in their own quiet detached way, although the younger brother was the knight-errant and showed much, much more bravado, rashness, than the Short One. One would suspect that the young one was the "give-me-the-strength" kind, for he was as big and tall as the other one was short, lean and slender. Indeed, he was destined to become the strong man of his tribe and along the entire coast as far north as the legendary shores of Sitka.

It was still very early, the people were coming into the lodge in a steady stream, whole families staying close together. Unobserved the Short One with his big partner rose from their places where they had been helping to stoke the great fires and went outside with the old man with the black cane, but who presently returned into the lodge and stood next to the entrance, evidently waiting for someone. In time he spoke to a man showing more excitement than he was wont to betray. The man went to his seat but rose and unobstrusively went the rounds among his home people whispering to them, without stopping. One by one the people, mostly young men and women, left the lodge without being noticed.

The business of the new day went on. The morning entertainment was taken over by the women members of the clan that was sponsoring the great Tloo-qwah-nah. They sang a long array of beautiful soothing songs, they did the undulating Dance of Gladness with the comely younger women of the tribe swaying to and fro, their arms out-stretched with the palms of their hands up, offering, giving out goodwill, generosity, human kindness to all present.

The undulating, inundating impression thus created in the firelight was pleasing for the eye to see, soothing for the soul to feel, to perceive — so much so that many who were sitting watching rose to join in or lead another group. They were a happy singing people. There was always something being shown, being sung, being told and the feasts became more plentiful, more lavish as the Tloo-qwah-nah progressed towards its end.

The Tse-shahts, sponsors of the Tloo-qwah-nah belonged to a large powerful clan with direct affiliations through past marriages, ancestry and alliance with ten distinct tribes along the length of the great island. Their founder had returned home to his mother's origin of birth from yet another powerful tribe south of the island and had founded this clan and named it, The People with Dwellings Under Their Seas. With his fearless leadership and hard work, the clan had grown and waxed strong, increasing in numbers and in wealth.

Their name, which the founder had retained and brought back from his father's land to the south could be interpreted as, The Whaling Clan. So the clan became great whaling people — one of the greatest along the entire coast of the land. They produced the most fearless warriors, the greatest speakers, mentors, artisans, singers and dancers. Frequently their services were sought to mediate and settle disputes or pass judgment in both domestic and political affairs.

Indeed the present speaker of the tribe belonged to this clan as did the master of ceremonies, the old man with the black cane. Though the founder was dead and gone four of his younger sons were alive and were all active in their respective roles as leaders in their chosen fields of endeavor. In his early youth the youngest of the four sons had made a name for himself and in his way he was as important as his eldest brother who was the most renowned sea-otter hunter. The others were hunters or artisans of high repute. The Short One was the poet, the singer, the dancer.

XV

IT HAD BEEN AN ESPECIALLY LAVISH FEAST for the noon meal.
People from the great lakes up the river, the People Whose
Dwellings Sit Atop a Craggy Knoll, had brought down fresh
deer meat especially for this feast. The meat was roasted,
broiled and cooked under live red-hot coals and eaten immediately after scraping the burned black crust off. The children
loved this last dish the most, biting on the tender ribs and
crunching the cartilage-gristle ends which went to make strong
white teeth because of the hard chewing.

The People Whose Dwellings Sit Atop a Craggy Knoll
lived in and around the two big lakes up in the vast hills. They
had so much meat and fish that they did not need to come
down to the unpleasant humidity of the coast at all so they
stayed in their own territory and allowed no one to molest
them in their own complete life. Nevertheless, these people
were related to the hosts through intermarriage of long standing. They were now contributing, assisting, without having
been approached, towards the great Tloo-qwah-nah, in a
fashion hard to surpass. When they rose to lift their thunder-
drums they rose in one body and like their own saying they
lifted the foundations with their voices when they sang for
their tribe. This occasion was no exception. They showed
their most cherished To-pah-tis,* they rendered their sacred
incantations. The People Whose Dwellings Sit Atop a Craggy

*Mystical inherited rites.

142

Knoll indeed proved their own greatness in their own individual way, separately from the presiding sponsors of the great Tloo-qwah-nah.

From the distance the boommmm of the thunder-drums was heard, faintly at first but with mellow penetrating sound quickly increasing in volume. A member of the home tribe conveniently stationed near the great entrance of the lodge admonished the throng to be more attentive. Although everything within the hall was in order this was their way of announcing a new number or play. Listen, it is the song for the march. Oomb, oomb, oomb, oomb. The slow tempo of the marching song could now be heard stealing into the closed lodge. The song grew stronger and more vibrant as the marching singers approached the lodge. Oomb, oomb, oomb, oomb. The great doors opened abruptly with the last beat of the booming drums.

For a long, long moment nothing happened, no sound, no movement came. Then the intoning voice of the head singer was heard as he sang the first bars of the Dancing-in Song and at the given down beat of his eagle feathers the drums boomed forth their low mellow sounds. The song leader appeared moving in very slowly, backwards, as did the drummers when they also made their appearance, coming in two at a time. This was to remind the onlookers that the main show was yet to come. When the last of the drummers entered they fanned out, one moving to one side, the next going to the other side, leaving the head singer at the point of the wide V with four drums on either side of him. There was no break, no hesitation, the drummers followed their conductor perfectly. The song ended abruptly with a loud boom of the drums, to be picked up again immediately.

At the precise moment of the crescendo of the beat the leading dancer flitted in so swiftly and so silently that the thrilled onlookers caught their breath and held it for a long gasp. The lone figure alighted into the middle of the open space just short of the figure V made by the singer and his drummers but, apparently in an exhausted prostration, doubled over on one bended knee, his face to the earthen floor, his arms hanging limp, relaxed, showing no movement.

At the boom of a given beat he lifted his head to survey the immediate surroundings; his eyes saw nothing, his arms rose slowly. Still on his knees he assumed a stance of readiness, arms at an easy angle, the left forward, the other to his side, his eyes searching, searching for a possible intruder, but seeing nothing. Slowly, calmly, his body came to life with his dance — his muscles, the sinews of his arms, quivering momentarily before he rose from his prostrate position.

His movements were deliberate but fast in their flowing action when he shifted his weight from side to side as he advanced into the hall. His partner, strong and tall, came in with an upright posture, his legs bent and set wide apart, his arms shoulder high, his muscles gleaming in the dancing light of the open fires, always moving, advancing in perfect time with the measured beat of the thunder-drums. Boomm, boomm, boomm. He followed his leader, twisting, stretching, down, up, to one side, to the other, the movements were slow, flowing, continuous, with no stops to break or jar the easy rhythm. Boomm, boomm, boomm, boomm, now in anticipation of combat — then the final glory of victory.

The movements bespoke those of the panther, the mountain lion, for this dancer was said to have been inspired by its graceful fluid movements as his song implied.

> I know the Panta.
> I have been to his house.
> I have seen him move.
> I have seen him dance.

Slowly, steadily, the two advanced as more and more male dancers entered the great hall, all moving and swaying with the beat. The troupe advanced in an unbroken line toward the far end of the lodge. There were now a great number of dancers inside, each expressing in his own way the Dance of Victory — not necessarily victory over wars but more over the victory of one's own fears, weaknesses, foibles, jealousies and the dread of want.

The story was told in their movements — manliness by the very display of his physique exhibited to the best possible advantage in scanty attire and in every performable way pleasing to the eye. It was more than the expression of joy, it was a disclosure, a revealment, the unveiling and the acknowledgement of all blessings granted by He Who Provides. The prostration on the earthen floor meant I, a mere man, the sign of life and awareness, of preparedness; the lift of the face showed a quest for strength, the exhibition of that strength of body and mind in his innermost self and finally a quest for generosity. Here I am, my God has made my body strong, my heart staunch. I offer You my all, come walk with me in serving all mankind. This was the message extolled, not by words, but by the graceful movements of the Dance for Victory.

There now appeared the first female dancer, to be followed successively by the same number of males who were already in the open arena. The girls' movements flowed and subsided, their arms and hands were held high over their heads as they swayed to and fro, remaining upright as they slowly turned half way round then back, advancing, following the male dancers.

The singing was building up to a higher pitch, the thunder-drums boomed louder and louder. Booomm, booomm, booomm, booomm.

The line of dancers reached the centre of the hall. The tall man manoeuvred around the leader, The Short One danced directly to him hearing and seeing nothing else. He must stop acting, no more make believe, this was their new dance, they must both make it real — Tloo-qwah-nah. Yes, that was the idea, the purpose was to stop showing off, to get into the spirit — Tloo-qwah-nah.

As he reached the forefront directly ahead of his leader the thunder-drums boomed their loudest, the singing reached the highest pitch to pause abruptly as the song-leader intoned the words of the chorus that must be used.

> You know the Panta House?
> I know the Panta House
> I have been to the Panta House
> I have seen the Panta dance.

The tall one was now directly in front of his partner who was easing back to spring forward at him in a slow, stretching move like a cat — onto him, above, into a tight ball, over in one continuous somersault and so alighting on the balls of his feet. There was a long pause, a miss in the beat of the drums for the new manoeuvre, then picking up again, the dancers not missing a beat, pressing forward with the two leaders drawing and urging them on.

The head of the column had now reached the far end of the hall and had begun to circle back down the opposite side. The male performers veered inwards to make an inner circle while the slower moving female dancers continued to make the resulting outer circle, thus taking up the entire space with the fires in the middle. The last of the dancers had entered, the great doors closed quietly. The leading female dancer manoeuvred to complete the outer circle, the song-leader watched to end the song at the proper moment and so end it with a resounding beat. The troupe filled the dance area of the hall with their two circles.

The rest was brief, the song had ended because it was the Dancing-in number. Now the dance proper must commence, the song-leader started the new song almost immediately, the beat of the thunder-drums stopped only to swing into a different tempo — livelier, faster. This was the new dance, never performed or shown before, invented, introduced by the Short One with his partner the Tall One. The male dancers were stripped down to their loin-cloths, with bright tufts of feathers dangling down from the elbows and red and yellow strands of beaten inner cedar bark streaming down from and around their wrists, knees and ankles.

And the female dancers showed off their womanly charms, their cheeks daubed attractively with red ochre, their deep set eyes severely shadowed black and their narrow eyebrows arched and pencilled provocatively. This was indeed a daring new dance, far removed from the proper, the staid, expected movements, or the wild abandon of the war dance.

Now the two leading dancers were in the centre of the inner circle. In this number there was a noticeable pause or miss in the beat at which time the star dancers executed their somersault routine. The approach or the beginning of the flip was hardly ever the same twice in a row, sometimes the Tall One would slowly and deliberately bend backwards, arching his back until his hands touched the floor and his partner would flip off his braced shoulders or from his bended knees.

Each dancer was now performing to the dictates of his own emotions and innermost feelings but keeping to the stretching, twisting up, down, to and fro movements.

> Do you know the Panta?
> I know the Panta.
> I have been to his house.
> I have seen him move.
> I have seen him dance.

Every move was guided by the throb of the thunder-drums. Boomm, boomm, boomm, boomm.

The performers executed a complete round and as the leading female dancer reached the far end of the hall again she stopped her advance and manoeuvred so that she faced the throng, swaying to and fro, shifting slowly and gracefully to her right as the other dancers pressed relentlessly toward her and with the slowing beat of the drums sidling to form an arc. While the male dancers now manoeuvred to form the inner arc the two leaders remained in the centre of the resulting crescent. The two lines contacted and tightened as the song came to a resounding end. All the performers were now facing the throng.

The third and last part of the performance was now in position. The head singer introduced the next song. It was a new one, never heard before. It was the song the Short One heard on the wings of the wind from the north that morning at the estuary before the beginning of the Tloo-qwah-nah.

The Wind. You E-ehe You E-ehe Ahye He ha La He-he. . . .

With a slow tempo it started, the formation of dancers began swaying sideways to and fro, the men swaying one way while the women swayed the opposite way. As the new song went its full length the high pitched humming filled the lodge with its long-drawn-out notes, the drums grew louder and faster with the singing until it turned into a stomp as the singers swung into yet another song. The stomp became heavier and more pronounced. The stretch, the sway were gone. Boom-boom-boom-boom-boom. The men in the front row of the column began a light hop, up and down on the balls of their feet. Gradually they assumed a squatting stance keeping both arms at shoulder height and leading with their left arms and gradually turning until their right arms were to the fore while the whole column advanced towards the onlookers to the front of the great hall. The women followed and stood waving their gaudy feathered bannerets in front of them. By the time the company had reached the edge of the arena near the sitting spectators the men were hopping up and down on their haunches, to rise again to their full height, reaching, reaching as high as they could, now shifting their weight from one leg to the other as they waved their arms side to side, to settle gradually towards the floor again as they executed the retreat, all waving their arms sideways until they reached their starting point. At that time the song ended on a moderate beat. Oomb. The dancers dispersed, disappearing behind a large screen while the old man with the black cane announced, "That was The Short One and his partner, Nah-tleet."

There was absolute silence amongst the spectators during the entire performance. All the children sat fascinated by the colorful costumes, especially those of the women dancers. To them all the dance was so different; it was full of action, yet it was slow and easy. Unlike the war dance which was loud, fast, arousing, maddening, this dance soothed, satisfied and entertained.

Many of the adults were offended, even repulsed, by the drastic departure from the long-standing and accepted fixed, prearranged and expected movements of the various existing dances. To be sure, there were many, nevertheless, to whom each dance represented some existing product or imitated children of nature so that each and every one of the numerous dances was readily recognized and its movements anticipated. This new dance was intended to win over men and women and urge them to greater heights of generosity so the dance required the men to show off manly supple bodies while the women showed their colorful costumes, using slow movements and coyness.

Representatives from the other tribes in this gathering took this new way of dancing with them to their own tribes and it was not long before they too produced their own versions. It was destined to become the most popular type of dancing along the west coast as more and more colors were introduced into costumes. The stretching twisting movements have been maintained and have survived to the present era, even though the dancers who imitate those of long ago have lost all knowledge of the beautiful fluid motions of Panta, the mountain lion.

XVI

Choo Why.   Choo why tligh, Chah-ma-dah!
Twenty plus seven days ago on this day
You and your clan graced our beach with your craft.
Our House at that time lifted you aloft
Because you with your deeds have won our acclaim
We as one, in this House, salute you.

Continue on the course that you have chosen
You are indeed a source of inspiration
To our young who aspire to goals seldom reached.
At this time we ask, entreat you to stay thus to teach
Our young the morals that are far from shallow
The ideals that you have learned to follow.

At this time mere words fail us, we grow faint
Because the strength that you have shown is great
Know this and do believe, of you we request
Remain strong and strive harder in your quest
For all that is noble and good for the conscience
For this is the object of our ancient teachings.

Yea, many more thanks are due to you at this time
Though you have heard our songs and also our rhymes
You have seen us dance for you and your House
Because of your manhood you our spirits arouse
We thus acknowledge your deeds with this token
This House extends its hand to clasp your own.

Chah-ma-dah, this token of our esteem for your person
Bestowed upon you in good faith from the head of our clan
This craft we do pray will serve you well

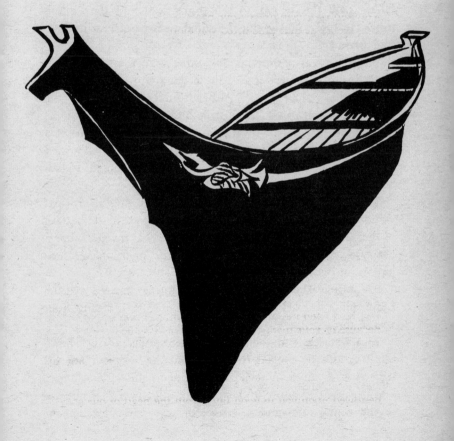

As you have served us without our call
We have sung with good heart now we would fain
That this sealing canoe you will call your own.

That with this craft you will yet increase
The store of food you provide from your seas
That Kí-tla-noose, the fur-seal, will beckon you on
That its lustrous robes will provide for your own
That you will throw the harpoon with arms that are strong
Tlah-coh, many, many thanks are due you from our clan.

WITH GREAT RESPECT AND ATTENTION the speaker of the House paid this tribute to the young leader of the visiting tribe. He spoke slowly and measured each word in a hushed, cool manner.

While he was addressing the young man the great screen made from the inner bark of the cedar tree was lowered, revealing the sealing canoe. A beautiful craft, made by the foremost artisan of the home tribe and given by the sponsor, the author of this Tloo-qwah-nah. Measuring four spans of a man it rested on two blocks of cedar, sleek and shiny, burned char-black, polished to a sheen, the insides painted Indian blood-red.

Two sturdy paddles made from yew lay on the thwarts while the water container and the bailer reposed in the bottom of the canoe on split-cedar matting. There was no spear, nor a harpoon, for tradition required that the uncle make these important items.

An audible Haaaaaaaa! escaped from the throng when the beautiful craft was unveiled and for awhile a steady hum waved through the crowd.

This was a gift in good faith, as the speaker of the House implied, and no official response from the recipient nor his tribe was required in such a case. But in this circumstance, and because the nature of the gift and as it was a total surprise to the young man and his tribe, the element of excitement crept in, not only amongst the recipient clan but with the entire throng. The great fires blazed merrily on their hearths, great sparks billowed up and through the open smoke-holes.

An immense silence filled the lodge as a man rose and moved forward and on to the earthen floor. He was an imposing man. Tall, big, barrel-chested, a man that had seen many seasons. His hair was thick but as white as the surf upon the outer rocks of his home to the south of the great Island. For a long moment he stood silent, his head bowed, his face inclined towards the earthen floor of the lodge.

Slowly, reverently, he raised his head and looked up, past the great beams and beyond the ridge. To him no vaulted roof impeded his vision from the source of his strength.. The lump that threatened to choke him with emotion subsided. Now he was bold and strong again. With a voice that rang to the rafters of the great lodge he rendered his invocation, pronouncing and emphasizing the gnomic implications of the words therein. He took his time, he hurried not. The rattle he shook was heard only between the bars or sentences of his chant, his voice was so rich and strong.

From the direction of the women's section of the home tribe an extremely high note issued forth, Kah-hh-haaaaaaaa-aaaaaa, to accompany the big man's prayer-song. It was rendered to form the background, it was an acknowledgement from the home tribe of the young recipient's response made through his uncle. The high note did not interfere, but rather enhanced the effect of the solemn proceedings. When he finished, the big man turned briefly to the young one, his nephew, and addressed him before he faced the councillors' quarters again.

> Stay, remain seated, nephew mine.
> This is a responsibility of our line.
> The labors, the deeds, the achievements shown
> Are reflections of your sires made known.
> In your youth you have made our House strong.

He with dwellings under his seas and your clan,
This House from whence you sprang,
Whose name you carry with honor and with fame,
Will stand and say Tlah-coh* without shame.
It is true we live apart at this time
Your House and my House will be one for some time.

Yea, our people from the south will stand again
We will stand as one for the son of our clan.
From our hearts we give thanks amain
The hand you extend we will clasp
When we stand forth to receive your prize.
How else can we say Tlah-coh but with praise?

Besides being one of the most influential and powerful tribes along the entire coast of the great Island, these people from the south, the Nee-tee-nah-ahts, were reputed to be the best trained and most talented singers and possessed a marvellous array of songs.

At this Tloo-qwah-nah they were indeed well represented. Their best men and women in every class or category of pursuits relevant to their life were about to show the strength of their House by their inherent talents with a vehicle that was unquestionably understood and accepted as the most satisfactory and convincing method or proof — the song.

With relatives from the home tribe, including sponsors of the Tloo-qwah-nah, one hundred strong stood up to sing the Song of Gratitude of the people from the south. Twenty thunder-drums boomed out along with the vibrant voices. One hundred voices swelled to a pitch that lifted the very foundations of the great lodge.

Eight stalwart braves from the tribe from the south slowly marched to the craft, four on each side, and very carefully lifted it a few inches off its blocks and put it down again. The beautiful canoe was now considered to be the young man's own.

The old man with the black cane strode to the middle of the

*Thank you.

154

arena, raised his cane high over his head and good naturedly declared, "Choo, we are bested again."

They were a happy singing people.

Other rituals were shown and performed for the remainder of that day. Ancient songs were sung with might and main. Thunder-drums boomed and throbbed with much zeal, perhaps to stave off the inevitable that was drawing near, ever nearer, by the fleeting moments of this, the evening before the last day.

Genie-aht, a pair of ancient masks of a male and a female were shown. They represented the giant people of the mountains. There was no dance or play attached to these masks. It was said that the giant people of the mountains were so far removed from all human life that no one had ever seen or known them dance. It was said that the originator of the masks had seen the pair of giants many generations ago and had carved their likenesses in cedar which became his To-pah-ti.* Throughout the generations they had ceased to be called masks and had acquired their own names and thus became an institution — Genie-aht, the giant people of the mountain. Now the Genie-aht were moved and paraded behind a screen.

Fires on the hearths were waning low. The time to put away all things for the day was at hand. Many compliments were heard from the guests of this great Tloo-qwah-nah. Though the compliments were directed to and were meant for the entire activities and portrayals of the day the effect of the new way of dance as shown by the Short one and the Tall One evidently remained uppermost within the guests' minds. The dramatic presentation of the new way to portray one's innermost feelings of benevolence, and the desire to share it with one's fellow man deeply affected the people as was evident in their glowing faces.

The throng did not rise from their seats, even though the fires were dying on the hearths and the chill from the outside

*Mystical inherited rites.

air was creeping in from all sides of the great lodge. They all sensed that the end must come and they were reluctant to hasten it. The hour was very late.

Twenty plus seven days had come and were dissolved into the mist of time. It was incredible the speed with which the invisible wings of that unrelated paradox could hide and carry forward that thing called time, so very unrelated to the Indian, the people of the west coast of the great Island.

They lived from one day to the next, they accepted all things as they came. They spoke slowly, they took much time before uttering, before replying, before expressing an opinion. When it was necessary to journey in their canoes to far-off places, they paddled because it took more time. The thick black hair upon their heads stayed blacker, longer, and did not shed and fall off.

Ah yes, to those people, time meant little, if considered at all. Yet time was never on their hands. They never sat idle for the sake of sitting idle. When the artisan sat doing nothing for hours, for days, he was really planning, formulating, or wrestling with a problem in his mind. Indeed, he made no start on any project until all the details had already been completed within his mind, so at times he sat for days ostensibly doing nothing.

XVII

It was a cold clear morning. There was no wind to be felt from any direction, the wind from the north slumbered in the hills. It was the last day for the Moon of Little Sister. Though none of the humans in the village could see her crescent she was still up there but she would retire to let her Big Brother take over. But then the people from other tribes from afar would be all gone. The oomb of the thunder-drums would not be there any more to measure and keep time for the songs and the chants, so really she was happy to go away for the season.

The sun loomed big and strong above the arête to the east. It pulled itself up past the snags and the barren maples across the river with no difficulty. There was no mist nor fog to reach up after it. It rose fast and was soon up above the tall trees to shed its rays on to the river which was high and still rising.

The Moon of Little Sister brought the highest tides of the entire season. The surface of the river was perfectly calm, so much so that a thin film of ice was forming along the banks and close to the shores on either side of the river.

The great canoes were pulled up above high-water mark, their cedar-bark mats hoary with the night frost; no one had come down to clean them off in readiness for possible emergencies. There would be plenty of time for that on the morrow when the guests began to prepare for their journey home. There would be plenty of time.

The throng had been in the great lodge since the early dawn. The fires were burning with vigor, the wood piled high, the draft sending the live sparks up through the open smoke-holes. There was a distinct warm air that could be felt throughout the vast hall. Everyone was in high spirits.

The naked sun was climbing fast, now approaching its low winter zenith, towards Yooksah-uh from whence the south wind comes.

Things were lagging within the great lodge. Perhaps the hosts had shown all they had to show, perhaps they had run out of To-pah-tis.* Maybe everybody was tired and anxious to be done and away to their own homes. Things within the great lodge were indeed lagging, except for the four fires everything else appeared dismal in the hall. Dutifully the women-folk gathered around and tried to liven things with their Dance of Gladness, but with little success.

The old man with the black cane and his immediate helpers were nowhere to be seen, although they had all reported into the lodge the first thing in the morning. Where was everybody? A fine time to be absent when everyone responsible was so desperately needed during this, the last day of the great Tloo-qwah-nah.

These were the feelings of the few people who were less informed. There was, and always will be, the small minority who under any circumstances find fault and remain unhappy, so there lurked the thought, "This may have started in a big way, but it certainly shows no indication of a decent finale."

Whhoooooooooooooo. . . .

It was the long-drawn-out call of Qwha-yha-tseek, the wolf. The call that struck fear into the hearts of all people of the coast. It came from a great distance but its high dismal note

*Mystical inherited rites.

entered and penetrated the cedar-plank walls of the lodge. No one spoke. No one moved. There was fear within the lodge. Where were all the menfolk? "We are being invaded by the Wolf People."

Whhooooooooooooo. . . .

The answering call came almost immediately. It came from the woods across the river and it was a loud, cold-chilling, blood-curdling call.

The fires within the lodge blazed merrily sending forth great sparks up and through the open smoke-hole.

"Outside, outside. Get outdoors, outdoors, outdoors, outdoors everyone!"

The elder sister, the matriarch, was by the great door of the lodge urging the women and children to get outside first. In a short time the area in front of the great lodge was filled with people standing expectantly and spilling out to the extreme bank of the river. No one spoke. There was fear everywhere.

The tide in the river was very high. Little Sister had brought the tides that flooded into the roots and boles of trees. The grass around the lower banks was all under water. This was the highest tide of the year.

The sun looked small and far away, reluctant to leave the horizon to the south. It shone directly onto the small patch of reeds that was still visible in the green across the river. The first wolf appeared from the woods onto the green patch of rushes above the high water. Without stopping, without a look to the left or to the right, the beast leapt into the waters and began to swim powerfully upstream. Other wolves followed the leader each leaping in and moving rapidly up the river with the tide that was washing and cleansing the roots and the boles of the trees along the river bank. There were nine of the great beasts in the water. There was one wolf missing!

There should have been ten wolves. Ten wolves were seen on that fateful day when the village had been invaded and ten Us-ma, children, were abducted and taken to the land of the Wolf People for four days.

"Where is the tenth one?" This question was asked by the matriarch because the menfolk were still absent. "Where is the tenth wolf?"

There was a commotion across the river where the other beasts had emerged from and presently a lone figure appeared. He was upright. He was a man. He moved with great difficulty in his efforts to reach the water so that he might leap in also and follow the rest of his comrades who were now moving upstream rapidly with powerful strokes. When the upright figure came into full view it was seen that he was pulling mightily on a stout rope tied to his middle and that he was being held back by something at the other end.

With mighty heaves the figure gradually pulled into view a big man who held onto the other end of the rope and thus prevented him from leaping into the frigid waters of the river as the wolves had done. The big man at the far end of the rope wore around his head, waist, wrists, knees and ankles the prickly green of spruce branches. That was, as the people knew, to ward off any evil that might otherwise befall the human who dared to intrude or otherwise find his way into the haunts or company of the Wolf People.

The big man had a magnificent build of body that stood forth in spite of the distance across the river. He leaned against the pull of the heaving man-thing with his might and main to prevent him from leaping into the icy waters of the swollen river. In spite of his gallant efforts the big man was losing ground, slowly but surely the man-thing heaved his way towards the edge of the sloping bank of the river thrusting out his long lean but muscular arms towards the water as if to pull it towards himself. Weaving to the right, then to the left because of the restraining rope, of which he seemed oblivious, he made no effort to undo it to free himself. All the time he inched nearer to his goal, heave, heave, pull, clawing the empty air with both hands, pulling the waters towards himself.

His bare feet were now within inches of the waters. Heave. His feet were in. He was in the water, ankle deep, heaving resolutely as he leaned forward, dug his right hand into the frigid waters, and with a great effort pulled his cupped hand up and splashed water onto his head and face while his left arm stretched far outward to maintain balance. When he had doused himself thoroughly, the man-thing stopped heaving and the big man on the other end began to regain lost ground by leaning far backwards. The rope was now around his shoulders. Encouraged by having stopped the man-thing at the brink of his goal, the big man dug his huge feet into the sandy soil and, leaning far backwards, began to inch himself and his captive back up the incline and thus back into the woods just as the last of the nine other wolf-men disappeared around a bend in the river.

Whhooooooooooo. . . .   Whhooooooooooo. . . .

It was the last two calls of the Wolf People.

"Canoes, canoes. Somebody get a canoe in the water!"

The matriarch called to no one in particular because the menfolk were still nowhere to be seen. The old man with the black cane was in the midst of the people and without speaking he raised his black cane high above his head. In an instant all the young men of the village appeared from all directions and instantly the open space nearest the beach where the canoes were kept under their mats was alive with young men eager to carry out whatever orders might come from their respected superior. The old man with the black cane, without words, motioned his men towards the great crafts and in a matter of movements the cedar-mats were lifted off the canoes revealing clean, dry crafts with paddles resting on thwarts in readiness for instant use. They were carried into the waters of the river and were off up the stream in pursuit of the Wolf People who had disappeared around the bend in the river. With four stalwart men in each canoe they raced up the swollen river and soon disappeared around the bend also.

The throng, the guests and the home people, pushed their way to the very brink of the bank of the flooded river. This affair was something new to all of them. Wolf-men leaping into the waters they expected and understood, because this was part of their law, but why the tethered one? Why the tenth one, the last one, why?

No one dared to ask this question outright. Certainly it must be a To-pah-ti,* that had never been shown or used by anyone else — to anyone's knowledge. The people from this river were daring resourceful individuals.

This observation was not voiced by the guests from the nine tribes along the coast of the great Island for it was considered beneath their dignity to manifest undue emotion when ceremonial rites were being shown. If the owner of the To-pah-ti wished to reveal the meaning thereof, or not, it was his and only his prerogative. This they all knew and understood.

Presently one of the canoes that had pursued the Wolf-men reappeared from the bend, the men paddling slowly, stalling, ostensibly awaiting the other crafts' return.

One by one the great canoes appeared around the bend. The man on the bow of each craft was standing and not paddling at all. The one at the stern did all that. He kept his sturdy paddle in and under the waters all the time during all the strokes, turning the blade deftly edgewise in order to make another pull. That method of paddling permitted complete control of the craft at all times. In that way the man could paddle and steer at the same time.

The great canoes approached the landing, taking much time, coming in prow first, and when they touched ground the old man with the black cane motioned again to the waiting men ashore who waded into the cold waters of the river. In pairs they approached the crafts, keeping to the right side of the canoes. Slowly, solemnly, the first pair leaned forward,

*Mystical inherited rites.

reached into the bottom of a craft and with a visible mighty lift heaved onto their lowered shoulders the body of a man-thing.

As each pair straightened up, spanned across them was the rigid form of a man. The nape of his neck was resting on the shoulders of the front man while his ankles were on the shoulders of the second man. In all appearances the man was lifeless and rigor mortis had set in. Thus the slow march up the incline of the beach and into the great lodge commenced, with the eight other bodies following close behind, all in the same unnatural span-across position, all without life, all stiff as solid beams.

No one made a sound. There was no chant. There was no incantation offered. No mother broke to run and see if the figure might be one of her own kith and kin. Fear gripped the hearts of those present to see and witness this tragic, un-believable scene.

The last of the morbid procession entered the great lodge and only then did the throng show any movement. Slowly it moved also, to follow, and when all had entered the great doors were shut tight.

Carefully, reverently, the apparently lifeless figures were placed on the earthen floor between, but not too close to, the two roaring fires that were still blazing at the middle of the hall.

The figures lay stiff. No steam rose or emitted from their cold bodies. They, to all appearances, were completely without life. Still no one spoke. No one made a sound or offered any explanation.

XVIII

THE FIRES ON THEIR HEARTHS were fast losing their glow. Big embers glowed eerily in the twilight of the early morn. The inside air was clear, there was no smoke in the lodge. No one stirred, there was silence everywhere.

Immediately after the last prostrate figure had been placed on the earthen floor with the other eight rigid men a pulsating, almost inaudible, roll of the ceremonial rattle was felt. It was perceived rather than heard. The roll, if indeed there was one, was a long way off. The faint sound seemed to drift down — perhaps through the narrow slit of the smoke-hole directly above the prone figures on the earthen floor. The eerie melancholy sound seemed suspended and refused to venture down past the great beams of the lodge. The roll was slow, so much so that it was almost a beat, one could almost count the pebbles in the rattle that produced the feeble rolling sounds. It seemed to last a long, long time and when it finally died away the eerie sounds of the languishing roll persisted and were reluctant to leave the mind. Embers on dying hearths struggled silently to remain alive with blue and purple glow. No one moved. There was silence everywhere.

Presently, from the direction of the inner chamber a distinct roll of the ceremonial rattle was heard for the second time. This time it was much stronger and evidently strove for more intensity, more volume. To be sure, it was still weak, but audible. It was real. Although its duration was no less than the first time it seemed to have just begun when it again trailed off into silence, to start again in a forceful vibrant roll.

From the still and dim atmosphere of the inner chamber there appeared a tall figure. Around his head, elbows, waist and ankles were the young green boughs of spruce. He moved slowly and deliberately, his eyes were fixed straight in front of him, his head held high — so high that his eyes were looking up and past the great beams of the lodge. He faltered not in his slow approach to the area where the prone and apparently lifeless figures lay on the dank earthen floor. Except for his loin-cloth and the spruce boughs he was naked. Black paint, the badge of all members of the Tloo-qwah-nah Society marked his face, a single bold stroke on each cheek. He carried in his left hand the sacred rattle that he was moving up and down in time with his slow pace. There was no song, no chant, no invocation, no orison. Except for the slow beat of the sacred rattle there was no sound in the great lodge.

Following the imposing looking man, each adorned with sprigs of spruce boughs, were three figures; the matriarch to his right, the master of ceremonies, without his black cane, to his left; and finally a huge young man who guarded the small column, making four persons altogether.

The prone figures rested by the hearth nearest to the inner chamber so the actual walk was not long. The sound of the rattle trailed off again as the tall man reached the first figure on the earthen floor. His head held high, his eyes looking up and past the great beams of the lodge, the imposing man began the roll of his sacred rattle for the fourth and final time. Slowly, very slowly, the man lowered his eyes until his chin rested on his bare chest. The rattle was gathering strength in volume and in speed until it became a distinct roll. The ping of the pebbles against the dry, seasoned hollowed receptacle of the sacred rattle penetrated to all corners of the hushed lodge. Except for their eerie glow the embers on the hearths refused to shed light on the prone figures or on the four figures now standing over them who were silhouetted eerily against the subdued glow of the hearth directly behind them.

Slowly, silently, almost imperceptibly the leading man with the sacred rattle sank to his knees next to the first prone figure on the earthen floor and was seen to bend over him for a long moment. The roll increased in pace and in volume. The kneeling figure bent down and rose four times and on the last rise, still on his knees, his eyes again sought the realms over and beyond the great beams of the lodge. Thus he sat.

Save for the increasing rhythm of the rattle there was silence in the lodge. The inert figure on the earthen floor moved his head ever so slightly, to his left, to his right, as if to determine or find the source of the roll of the rattle. Slowly his eyes opened and when he could discern the kneeling figure beside him his head straightened so that he was facing straight up once more and there issued from his mouth a thin stream of water. It spouted up and back down splashing and thus washing his face. Now his limbs stirred. He sat up and his eyes sought the earthen floor of the lodge in humiliation for he must never forget that he was merely a part of Mother Earth.

In rapid succession the other eight figures were revived to apparent life with no break or variation in the procedure. All the young men upon being resuscitated stirred and moved their limbs before sitting up and standing in line immediately behind the man with the sacred rattle. The nine stalwart young men formed a half circle at the area's far end where the panel of councillors sat with the king of the Tse-shahts, the nation from the big river. The roll of the rattle trailed off into the distance and the man, with his sacred rattle poised silently waist high in his left hand, rose and deliberately turned to face the revived men while his three attendants shifted around to retain their original positions.

The old man, the master of ceremonies, lifted up his countenance and began calling out names. As each name was called one after another of the children who had been abducted by the Wolf People stepped forward willingly and formed a second half circle directly in front of the revived men. They came in their normal clothing with no spruce boughs adorning their bodies. When the tenth and last child completed the line the matriarch also raised her countenance while her own rattle came to life with its resounding roll as she commenced her invocation, her prayer chant, her orison. Her voice came strong and clear with the strength, the intensity, the sureness of her faith in a Power — the Creator that gave life to all growing things, including man. Her voice reached its climax as she lifted her head higher and her eyes looked over and beyond the great beams of the lodge before the rattle's roll tapered off and was lost in the far distance. There was silence in the great lodge. The erstwhile glowing embers now lay sombre on their hearths but remained alive, reluctant to trail off and die like the sound of the rattles.

THE NEW MEMBERS

Rulers, chiefs, queens, maidens and braves.
Here they are, Us-ma, the revered young of our tribes.
Lift now your countenances and gaze upon their faces
They were gone for awhile but returned with no harm.

Before and behind them stand the stalwart braves
Who forsook their pallets and slept not
Who turned their heads away from the fires in the lodge
Who ventured into the dark woods to find your Us-ma.

Who indeed donned the robe of the wolf and mingled
    with them
While you and I sat and sang beside the protecting fire
For four days, for four nights, the vigil lasted
There was no sleep, no food.　　No rest came to these men.

Though they came home with your Us-ma and also mine
To the call of the wild they could not say nay
So they donned the robe of the Wolf People once more
Stole into the dark woods and mingled with them again.

Qwha-yha-tseek, The Wolf

Yea, the call of the wild may be strong,
The urge to roam the forest with care unfettered
May be hard for the brave to deny
Yet the call of home and loved ones is stronger still.

It may be said that this call did reach these men
Though the robes of the Wolf People were upon their backs
Though they did mingle with them in the wood
Into the waters they plunged to escape the call of the wild.

To swim upstream for the waters to cleanse their bodies
From the smell of the people of the wolves
Until exhausted and prone, face down upon the waters,
They were rescued and borne as you saw.

All this they did because it is the law of our land.
One must not defile the home of the Us-ma of our band
With the smell from the den of the wolves.
All this we know and understand.

Rigid like flotsam from the river
Their bodies were carried into this lodge.
Cold, inert, their bodies lay upon the earthen floor
Hearing nothing, seeing nought.

Having cleansed their bodies with the waters
The man with the knowledge of medicine
Took compassion on their plight
Coaxed, stimulated life back into their limbs.

The man with the knowledge of medicine
Would remind us all that no mortal
Can give life to man or to beast.
This is the will of the Creator of all living things.

Stand now he who was tethered with the braided cord
Approach and move forward to rejoin your group
For the stout braided cord deterred you not
You washed your head, your face, we all saw.

For a purpose you were tethered, there is no doubt.
It is not ours to seek the answer now
This precedent you set will mark you well
Let no one else use the same in other plays.

The To-pah-ti* of the wolf with us you share
This knowledge is known throughout the tribes.
Hear now, a new To-pah-ti this day was shown
For all time this shall be yours alone.

Look now into the faces of the Us-ma who are yours
Who stand proud before you at this time.
Lift up your countenance, rejoice with us,
Count now the Ten that make the whole.

Let it be known throughout the tribes
The price these Us-ma have paid in full
Has made them one and all
Honored members of the Tloo-qwah-nahs.

The old man with the black cane was his jovial self again when he stood tall to deliver the explanation to the throng. The mirth in his ageing eyes glowed like the fire that was now being replenished with dry seasoned wood. Young men stacked the wood high to form its own chimney.

*Mystical inherited rites.

XIX

THE OLD ONE FONDLED HIS BLACK CANE rubbing it lightly with his right hand as he waited patiently for the young maidens who, under the direction of their leader, were now forming a line at the far end of the great lodge. The well-trained girls rapidly took their places in the line that would again make a wall of dancers and in a short time they were ready.

It was the same troupe that had performed and opened the ceremonies at the inception of the great Tloo-qwah-nah a full moon phase of twenty-eight days ago, but with the addition of four new dancers. On the extreme ends of the half circle and a little inward from the main line four little girls stood poised and ready to give their initial performance. Six little boys who were also initiated into the secret society of the Tloo-qwah-nahs followed the men singers and drummers to their positions a little to the back of the girls. This would complete their feeling of truly belonging to the House. This was the psychological moment when the child was coaxed to grow into the Tloo-qwah-nah frame of mind. This early manifestation of trust from the elders was to mean much to the child throughout his growing period and induce love and admiration in his young mind.

The old man with the black cane was indeed in high spirits. The crinkles at the corners of his eyes showed up pale and white against the black paint upon his cheeks that accentuated his deep-set eyes. Twenty-seven days had come and gone again. The twenty-eighth was at hand and already approaching noon. It had been a long session for him but he had not missed a day in his responsibilities as the official master of ceremonies. To be sure he had enjoyed every moment of it and would do it all over again as he had done throughout his long and fruitful years. Now this session was drawing to a close. Would there be others? He wondered. These thoughts ran through him as he paced slowly to the side of the great lodge so that he might not detract any attention from the throng.

Perhaps this was to end, to close, the great Tloo-qwah-nah. No one could say except the giver of the Potlatch. There was always that air of total expectation, that wondering feeling of what was coming next in the minds of the spectators. When you witnessed a new play or dance in the great Tloo-qwah-nahs you marvelled; when you saw a play that had been seen countless times before you enjoyed it because you had not known that it was to be shown. A simple philosophy that these people utilized again and again to its full extent.

The wall of maidens stood motionless with gaudy shawls draped around their shoulders. Their eyes were cast low upon the earthen floor of the now brightly lit lodge as the four fires stacked high with dry wood began to flame and crackle in the stilled air.

The song leader with the white feathers of the eagle began to intone the opening strains of the song. Except for his lone voice there was absolute silence in the lodge other than the hiss of the four great fires upon their hearths. The white feathers arrayed like a fan were lifted high and came down with vigor. At that precise moment the battery of thunder-drums boomed forth their mellow penetrating oomb! The Song of Joy and Gladness had begun.

Suddenly, without warning, two young men darted from behind the wall of dancers, their arms outstretched, their knees bent slightly as they pranced in, their steps and movements keeping time with the thunder-drums. Their hands were facing upwards in a grasping position and were filled with the down of the wild swan. With each beat of the drums the down escaped from their hands, drifting in the rush of air caused by their own moving bodies before settling on the earthen floor of the lodge. One pranced to one side of the arena while the other went to the opposite side and as they wheeled to come back a cloud of snow-white down filled both areas. Four times they wheeled and four times they met at the centre of the arena before the Song of Joy and Gladness came to a resounding end and both men darted back behind the screen of dancers.

The drums were silent for a moment. Then they boomed forth again and with the first beat the maidens swung to wheel from side to side in flowing movements, only to stop again for another brief rest. With the third song the four little girls detached themselves from the line and began dancing towards the centre swaying to and fro in the strewing motion and when the song ended they stood perfectly still in the middle waiting for the fourth and final number. When the song ended they were all back in their original positions at the ends of the half circle.

The maidens dispersed among the spectators, but the song leader and his singers and drummers remained where they were. The leader stood tall with his eagle feathers cleaving the air high above his head beating out a new tune — one-two-three, one-two-three — intoning in a rich voice the opening lines before swinging his white feathers down with an affected gesture so that his drummers would strike simultaneously a resounding boom on their tight newly warmed drums. The song stopped abruptly but the feather baton remained beating up high and when it swept down for the second time the song resumed. A high-pitched voice, a full octave higher, came in clear ringing tones, "Sing the chorus. You will now do the chorus. This you will say."

My land, my domain, the seas that are mine
Flow, yea overflow, with the oils
You will see, this you will see.
The oils fill my land till it does overflow.

Immediately the voice broke into the song the drums ceased, leaving the singers to follow the beat of the white eagle feathers. Simultaneously with the beginning of the last line of the chorus the drums broke in with a boom and with might and main the singers voiced, "The oils fill my land till it does overflow." The young men who had been standing nearby deftly poured flagons of whale oil on the fires until great flames leapt high licking the rafters menacingly as they burst through the open smoke-holes. Each time the song ended the feather remained in motion until the song had been sung the full four times.

In the meantime more and more men and women rose from the spectators' area to join the singers until the rafters reverberated. The wood chimneys for the great fires tumbled down as the final note of the song ended with a deafening boom of the thunder-drums. Once more there was silence everywhere within the lodge.

Slowly the main doors opened and fresh air gushed in, drawn by the warm humid air inside. The fires glowed in huge orange-red embers, only occasional weak flames escaping now and then. Silence reigned within the lodge. Young and old took deep breaths and retained the sweet air in their lungs as long as they could. This was indeed a welcome relief after the immediate tense moments.

The sun had broken through the morning fog that persistently hung low over the valley at this time of year in spite of the freezing nights. Hoar frost on the naked trees clung to their slender limbs intent on shielding them from the cold winds from the north.

Autumn floods had come and were gone again leaving a fine layer of sand on the low ledges along the river banks to protect the roots of the dormant grass from the freezing coldness of the winter frost that would build until it stood erect like ravaged limbs on a barren plain.

The great doors remained open. Shafts of sunlight intruded from the open smoke-holes above dying fires. A thin spiral of blue smoke rose from the hearth nearest to the door. A shaft of light coming through the opening accentuated by the blue smoke slanted directly to the immediate entrance inside the door.

The right side — the side away from the river — of the lodge, normally occupied by the home people had been quietly vacated and half the entire length of the hetsauk, the low platform that ran below and along the raised living quarters, had been removed and placed on top of the other half of the same platform to create a screen about two feet high that extended from the doors to the far end of the great lodge.

Pooffff!

The silence was broken by the distinct sound of a whale blowing in the distance.

Pooffff!

There it was again, clearly and distinctly the sound drifted into the lodge from the direction of the open doors.

Pooffff!

Blue smoke spiralled languidly from the fire nearest the open door. The forceful roll of a rattle intruded, followed immediately by a strong resonant voice.

> Yea, it is for the Power on High.   Yea, it is
> That I roam the sea in search, always in search.
> In the goodness it offers I search for the ultimate in food
> I search for Ee-toop,* bigness, largeness,
> The mass that moves upon the seas.
> Yea, it is for the Power on High.   Yea it is.

The voice trailed off in a long-drawn-out note until it died

*The whale.

out completely and there was silence everywhere.

Pooffff!

From behind the raised screen immediately inside the doors a black object appeared momentarily, only to disappear silently behind the screen, again moving forward in an up, down motion, amid total silence in the great lodge. After what seemed a long moment the prow of a whaling canoe appeared and moved into view. Slowly but surely it glided into full view.

Pooffff!

The great whale — for this is what the black object depicted — rose again. Heavily, laboriously, the great bulbous nose and head appeared into full view as it heaved forward. This time its elongated hulk came into sight before its relatively small dorsal fin appeared, directly under its base there was a deep gash from which oozed the red of its own blood and from the gash there was a taut rope extending backwards and so out of sight.

Pooffff!

Slowly the great hulk appeared again, its sides glistening in the weak fire-light from the dying embers. The whale heaved its length up to its dorsal but its great flukes did not show. They did not appear. This meant that the whale was not sounding, but swimming on the surface. It was under control. It was tethered. Great skin buoys appeared directly behind Ee-toop, the whale, to drag and help keep it under control.

Pooffff!

The whale, the taut line, the skin buoys all came into view and were gone again in the midst of the total silence that prevailed in the great lodge, and lo and behold there loomed into sight a big man. His great muscular right arm extended shoulder high in front of him. With his head held high, his eyes focused high up, above and beyond the great beams of the lodge. The taut rope was fastened to the thwarts at the prow of his whaling canoe. Into full view he moved, to be followed by his crew of eight stalwart men who held their sturdy paddles low and deep in the imagined waters to steady themselves and their great craft to the fullest possible extent. There was no need to paddle. The weight of the moving whale propelled them forward mightily. All occupants of the whaling canoe were motionless. No one turned, moved or pulled on their paddles. Blue smoke spiralled upwards from the dying hearths in search of the smoke-hole. There was silence everywhere.

The roll of the rattle broke into the silence again and the same rich voice rendered yet another incantation.

> To'ards the beach of my home that you know
> You will turn, paddle on, do not stop, paddle on.
> Ee-toop, bigness, largeness, the mass that moves
> Upon the seas, the salt-chuck that is mine
> To'ards the beach of my home that you know
> Paddle on, do not stop, paddle on.

The incantation was chanted in an even unchanging mono-tone, the chanter holding strong his mellow voice right up to the last bar when it gradually trailed off into the mythical seas beyond the shadows in the flickering lights from the dying embers on the earthen floors of the great lodge.

The progress of the dramatic pantomime and the movements were extremely slow as it moved down the long stage and yet it was nearing the far end too rapidly. Blue smoke spiralled upwards past the bright shaft of sunlight slanting down from the smoke-hole.

Pooffff!

Slowly, majestically Ee-toop rose from behind the screen, the dark red of its blood directly below the dorsal fin rolling and rippling ever so slightly from the draft created in the low passageway behind the screen. The taut rope never slackened, the figures never moved, the silence was unbroken, the melo-drama moved down the aisle in the subdued and hushed at-mosphere of the lodge.

Before, just before, it reached the far end of the long aisle the great mammal was seen to veer slightly inwards as if to change course to head for a given point. The small dorsal fin disappeared behind the screen and the huge flukes, appearing for the first time, were seen to move up and down in slow powerful strokes. Ee-toop was paddling itself onward.

The taut rope never slakening, the figures never moving, the silence unbroken, the drama lost itself into the darkness.

The erstwhile faint and languid embers began to glow with a resurgence of life, crackling and bursting on their hearths in an onrush of draft from an unknown source. In the direction where the moving drama had disappeared the eagle feather was cleaving the air high above the now deserted platform. The beat came fast and continuous. Boom-boom-boom-boom-boom.

All four fires were being stoked and replenished with dry cedar wood. The flames grew rapidly, licking upwards and sending out great sparks onto the earthen floor of the lodge. As the light in the end area increased the song leader emerged with his right arm raised high cleaving the air and beating time with his eagle feather which gleamed in the firelight. He was followed by his battery of drummers, eight in all. Four marched slowly to the far end on the left while the other four remained at the right end. The white feathers cleaved the air silently.

The singers, all men, filed into the now lighted area moving slowly until the entire end was filled with the large company of men. When the gleaming white feathers plummetted violently the battery of thunder-drums struck simultaneously with resounding, continuous beat and the new song, never before heard, stole forth into the still, tense atmosphere. The song began on a low note but gradually rose in pitch and in volume as the white eagle feathers rose higher and higher and the drums boomed louder and louder. After a few more vigorous beats the fan-shaped white feathers plunged down and there was complete silence in the lodge.

Now waist high the feather fan remained in motion and when it dropped the song resumed again on the low note, gradually building up and up. Well above the rest of the voices, in a penetrating pitch, the keeper of the song intoned, "Do the chorus now, you will now do the chorus. This you will say —"

> Swirling dust in the air
> From the road to my lodge never sets
> The seashell-flakes on the path to my door
> By the tread of coming men never sets.

Throughout the chorus the thunder-drums had lessened in volume until they were barely audible above the intoning voice. When the chorus had run its course the voice broke in again. "Repeat, you will repeat the chorus."

> Swirling dust in the air . . .

As the second round of the chorus commenced a wisp of down floated in on a current of air about knee high above the earthen floor. Without warning or words a figure draped in a robe of sea-otter eased himself from behind the screen of singers. He sidled and bobbed low on his haunches, his back was to the onlookers. Springing lightly, keeping time in accordance with the fast beat of the drums, the figure sidled to his left and rose gradually as he traversed the earthen floor until he was upright. As he turned the gaudy headdress of a sea-serpent, ornate with inlays of abalone shell for eyes, teeth and other markings, was revealed into the full light of the now blazing fires.

Boom-boom-boom-boom-boom. The dancer glided lightly on the balls of his feet. The sea-serpent figure proud and aloof, his head held high, surveyed the mythical seas to the horizon, looking, searching the four corners of the winds — the north, the south, the east and the west. Each movement of its head billowed out delicate clouds of down of the wild swan that floated up and around the dance area before being wafted down onto the earthen floor of the lodge. The dancer reached the far end of the area by moving anti-clockwise and when he turned to face the light showed the bold stroke of black paint upon his cheeks which extended into the hollow area of his deep-set eyes. He took rapid short steps as he glided along the hard packed floor, his movements simulating the fluid sinuous motility of the legendary serpent upon the surface of the sea. A proud and stately figure, gaudy, colorful in his markings, masterful in his mien. The message was bold.

I AM MASTER OF ALL THAT I SURVEY.

Again the song was repeated twice more until the full four times were complete when the whole presentation ended abruptly and most vigorously.

XX

THE FIRST HALF OF THIS THE LAST DAY of the great Tloo-qwah-nah had slipped by so rapidly and the throng were so engrossed in the entire proceedings of the morning, with its swift sequence of continuous movement of one drama after another that held them speechless with wonder, they had completely forgotten their hunger.

It was long past noon. The throng still sat motionless on the hetsauk that ran the length of the lateral walls of the lodge. The side that had been removed for the tethered whale panto-mime had been replaced and the home members of the tribe had quietly returned to their places.

The young men were already busy spreading the long cedar-bark mats in front of the people in preparation for the last meal. Other men appeared, entering through the still open doors of the lodge. Two men carried steaming ornate feast dishes followed closely by four younger men each carrying a smaller wooden bowl. Other teams followed until there were four teams each with similar steaming feast dishes. The first team went directly to the section where the king sat with his councillors and aides while the others went to serve the great throng. In a surprising short time the steaming food was being served all round.

In spite of the rigid training to keep one's composure and show no surprise an audible cry of approval sang out above the hum of the happy people. Hahhhhhhhh. Duck soup! Duck soup! Ho! ho! ho! ho! ho!

THE ACKNOWLEDGEMENT

Ahh-aye, ahh-aye.   Ahh-aye, ahh-aye!   So be it, so be it.
We have seen, we have heard.
It is they, it is they.   The Maukl-aye-aht!
It is the People With Dwellings Under Their Seas.

We have heard their songs,
We have seen their dances,
We have witnessed their plays,
At their To-pah-ti* we marvelled.

Heni-soo-ook, the tethered whale
Attests to their own greatness.
The whale means the opulence of their seas.
The rope, the tether, is his control.

The down of the swan
Offered to you and to me
Means friendship, trust and compassion
Above the alliance of the Ten Tribes.

Yea, it is they, the Nan-chim-wus-aht
The flukes of the whale adorn their great lodges
The whalers, the sea-otter and sea-lion hunters
Whose oils run and overflow their land.

.It was the speaker with the soft speaking voice who uttered
the words. He delivered his address quietly. Though he
directed his acknowledgement to the sponsors of the Tloo-
qwah-nah he turned slowly, counter-clockwise to the four
corners of the great lodge. This indicated, without his saying
so, that he was speaking for the entire throng. He said many
things more pertaining to the Tloo-qwah-nah, to the firm
solidarity of their alliance that made the Ten Tribes and the
resulting strength of such an alliance. The speaker with the
soft-speaking voice from the nation to the south of the great
Island, the Nee-tee-nah-ahts, said many things more. He
spoke slowly. He spoke for the entire duration of the last meal.

The people ate slowly, swallowing the food, imbibing words

*Mystical inherited rites.

of wisdom. The voice was low but it reached to the far corners of the great lodge. Soothing, penetrating like Kup-chah, the song the rapids sing; entreating, like the silent beauty of the pool below a waterfall; persuasive, like the wavelets on sands of inflowing tides whose sounds are felt beyond the bole of the great spruce in the wood.

In the great lodge the throng knew and felt that there was indeed authority in that quiet voice of the speaker from the south of the great Island. The people ate and drank in the words of wisdom.

The guests had eaten the duck soup with relish. Huge tureens, made from the bole of a maple, were replenished time and time again with the rich nourishing soup replete with big chunks of mallard and golden-eye meat that had been pre-singed on an open fire before being eviscerated and thrown into the huge cooking pots. From wooden goblets the children sipped and drank broth that was bubbling with its own natural fat until there was no more left in the huge wooden pots. Indeed there was little Mah-moot* after this meal.

In each locality along the coast the people were famed for their own species of fruit and specialized in its preservation. Tribes were known for their Yuh-ma, salal berries, salmon-berries, red huckleberries, or cinnamox, which are blueberries. Ca-wee, wild blackberry, was the fruit of the Tse-shahts. It was blackberries that ended this last sumptuous meal of the great Potlatch. Though they had been dried and kept through-out the past four moons they tasted fresh after being soaked in water overnight. Many cakes of this dried berry were taken home for the guest's Mah-moot.

The speaker with the soft speaking voice was still addressing the throng. He was now summing up his observations, ac-knowledging all that had transpired throughout the great Tloo-qwah-nah, reminding the throng that all events were in their proper place and that all had gone well. He ended his long oration with these words:

*Left-overs.

To the Tloo-qwah-nah we do assemble
To frolic, play and make merry
To cast off our cares to the winds from the north
To extend the hand of friendship to each other
To review our laws and our tenets
To cement alliances closer together.

The throng ate slowly, swallowing the tangy dessert and imbibing the words of wisdom that came from the speaker with the soft speaking voice. Ten drums had been placed on the hetsauk immediately in front of the king's inner chambers. Ten representatives, one from each tribe, presided over the drums that were placed flat on the raised floor of the hetsauk. These drums served as a desk or table from whence the names of all attending guests were issued to the representatives of the host. Each guest received a Pa-chuck, or present. Every representative knew exactly who and how many were attending from his own tribe and because of their renowned retentive memories no member or delegate was ever missed.

As a rule the disposal of visiting tribes was dealt with without undue ceremony and the tribes from the greatest distance were taken care of first. As each tribe was discharged its representative and his drum was removed, and so on until all had been served with their Pa-chuck. Each present was alluded to as a token, a portion, a wisp of down issuing forth and descending from the affluence of the land and sea that belonged to the giver of the great Tloo-qwah-nah.

As each name was called the person stood up but was not obligated to step forward to receive his present and waited for a steward, appointed for these special occasions, to bring it to him. This deference was given at all Tloo-qwah-nah ceremonies because all persons were deemed to be special guests and were never subjected to embarrassment however slight. In other feasts and ceremonials when the giving of the Pa-chuck was in progress the recipients were obliged to stand up, come forward and offer Tlah-coh* in a loud clear voice.

*Thanks.

While their men were immersed with protocol the women quietly and without ado began distributing their own wares and offerings amongst the entire gathering, leaving the home people to the last. All members, both male and female, connected to the House involved with the Tloo-qwah-nah served as stewards, ushers and helpers so that the whole business of the Potlatch was dispensed with speedily.

Though the actual Tloo-qwah-nah had ended the host's obligations for this Tloo-qwah-nah was not yet at an end. Conditions, terms, articles of agreement and laws still must be adhered to and satisfied. One year from the termination of the ceremonies of the Tloo-qwah-nah the host must recall his own tribe and give another feast to properly put away all ritual songs, dances and paraphernalia used during the Tloo-qwah-nah. That was the law as laid down by ancient forebears.

XXI

The morning dawned clear and crisp
There was no cloud in the pale blue sky
The tide filled the river in the early morn
The sun arose over the arête to the east
Yoo-ah-ti nudged the rime off the naked trees
It sparkled on the breath of the wind from the north.

THE GREAT CANOES, not bound together as they had come, were now leaving, swinging in a wide arc and disappearing into the bend in the river with their paddles flashing against the early morning sun.

The Short One stood alone on a landing below the great lodge. He had been helping the young chieftain with his departure in his new sealing canoe that he had acquired at the Tloo-qwah-nah. Now the beautiful canoe was moving downstream also, the young stalwart chieftain at the stern, his wife in the centre and their young son at the bow looking backwards and waving good-bye to the lone figure on the beach.

This was the end. There was no more. The Short One stood forlorn and motionless as he watched the last canoe move downstream and fade into the mist.

EPILOGUE

CHAH-MAH-DAH

HEIR APPARENT OF THE TSE-SHAHT PEOPLE

He was a big man   An imposing man.
His limbs were lithe, lean and strong.
There was pride in the way he moved.
Slow and lazy, like the stream that runs deep.
There was no room for arrogance in his face.
It smiled to all men and also to nature.
His hair was long and luxuriant.
It glistened in the night.
The moon coaxed rich glints of color,
Like old cedar, rubbed smooth with bark of its own.
His dark eyes were set wide.   They were alive,
Like the charred black planks above the fire.
When he turned, the color, the hue of his skin shone,
Like the copper in the light of a growing moon.
His sea-otter breech cloth glistened in the night.
He stood naked before his God, Creator of all men
He spoke with ease.   There was no hurry.   The night
    was long.
He need not say that he was kind, that he was good.
No need to tell that he was generous, truthful and
    honest too.
No boasts of arms so strong, of will power secure.
Long years of training, of bathing in the streams of a tarn;
Rubbing, kneading and scouring his limbs with the herb
    of yew.
From a child to manhood he was in commune with
    the Creator
His mien, the tilt of the head, bespoke the strength
    of body and of will.

Now in early manhood, he stood before Him.
With pride, adoration he held his head high.
His hair tied in a knot atop the crown of his head
No shadow, no hair impeded the eye, the face he offered
  to Him.
He had seen a score plus ten and five of winter snows.
He was a man, rooted to earth.   To mother earth.
He was the Chah-ma-dah, heir apparent.
He would succeed the king, he must remain strong.
Four days have come and gone again.
This was the fourth night of a crescent moon.
He had cleansed his body, his mind and his heart
In his pool in the mountain tarn.
He was ready, he was willing, he spoke directly to his God,
"Huh-walth, King of Creation, grant me the will, the desire,
The generosity, the wisdom to finish this my duty at hand."
  Choo, uhh-ahh, Amen.
The crescent moon shone and twinkled in the heavens.